The Poor and the Good News

A Call To Evangelize

Edited by
Tom & Lyn Scheuring
with
Marybeth Greene

PAULIST PRESS
New York and Mahwah, N.J.

Library of Congress Cataloging-in-Publication Data

   The Poor and the good news : a call to evangelize / edited by Tom
and Lyn Scheuring with Marybeth Greene.
     p. cm.
   ISBN 0-8091-3359-8
   1. LAMP Ministries. 2. Church work with the poor—Catholic
Church. 3. Church work with the poor—New York Region.
4. Catholic Church—New York Region—History. 5. New York
Region—Church history. I. Scheuring Tom. II. Scheuring, Lyn.
III. Greene, Marybeth.
BX2347.8.P66P66 1993
282'.7471—dc20
                                              92-37976
                                                 CIP

Published by Paulist Press
997 Macarthur Boulevard
Mahwah, New Jersey 07430

Printed and bound in the
United States of America

Contents

A Closer Look

APPRECIATIONS

The Poor and the Good News is written to give witness to the compassionate love of our Father, through Jesus, in the power of the Spirit, especially for the "anawim," the poor, in this the tenth anniversary year of LAMP. It is dedicated to the poor, who also evangelize us. We honor St. Joseph, patron of the universal church, who has continually provided for us, and Mary, mother of the church, who intercedes, who is ever "in labor" till our hearts beat with the heartbeat of God for the coming of his kingdom in love and justice.

We thank the LAMP ministers for their accounts of evangelization in this book, and Maria, Malissa and Paul Scheuring for their assistance and constant willingness to foster Lamplighters' service among youths. We are most grateful to Cardinal John J. O'Connor for his consistent encouragement and for his particular concern for LAMP's ministry with homeless families. We express special gratitude to Bishop Joseph Francis and Bishop Francisco Garmendia for their guidance and inspiration at the very beginnings of LAMP as well as throughout the last ten years. Among others who have profoundly affected our journey of faith, and to whom we are deeply grateful, are Fr. John Randall, Fr. Leo Courcy, and very especially, our parents. Remembered in the dedication of these pages is the late Alvin Illig, C.S.P. (a Paulist priest and pioneer in the area

1

of evangelization in the United States), who was always an encouraging support, especially for his help in our founding LAMP. Foremost in our gratitude to God is our associate director, Marybeth Mutmansky Greene, whose faithful love for the Lord and his poor has been indispensable in the fruitful evolving of LAMP.

Please note: Out of respect for our brothers and sisters in material poverty, be aware that in this text, their actual names are either changed, or only first names are printed.

FOREWORD

Of the many movements which have emerged in the Church since the Second Vatican Council, perhaps none is more aptly named than LAMP Ministries, for it is a shining beacon of hope in the midst of a world desperately in need of the Gospel. Since its beginnings, this unique work has sought to bring the message of Christ to the everyday lives of the poor who are in the most difficult of situations.

Tom and Lyn Scheuring, the founders of LAMP Ministries, are two of the most extraordinary people I have ever met. Witnessing to the faith in every action of their lives, Tom and Lyn are a remarkable couple, parents of remarkable children. Reading these pages will give you but a hint of the depth of the dedication which they have shown to the Church and which has benefitted God's people in countless ways. As you will read, this has not always been easy for them.

Firmly rooted in a deep conviction that God would not fail them, Tom and Lyn with the LAMP staff have worked selflessly toward the spiritual success of this ministry. Serving in materially poor parishes, schools, with the homeless and other evangelistic outreaches, LAMP Ministers are people filled with the unique joy that comes from knowing that the light of Christ can never be extinguished. It is my hope that those who read the words of this book will be inspired to follow them and so become the light shining in the darkness.

John Cardinal O'Connor
Archbishop of New York

INTRODUCTION

"Unrolling the scroll . . . Jesus found the place where it is written: The Spirit of the Lord has been given to me, for he has anointed me. He has sent me to bring the good news to the poor; he has sent me to heal the broken-hearted and to proclaim liberty to captives and to the blind new sight, to set the downtrodden free . . ." (Lk 4:18).

In the early years of our married life (late 1960s and early 1970s), while frequently reflecting on the life of Jesus, we were often amazed as to how much Jesus reached out to the poor, the outcast, those whom everyone else rejected. We noticed that he reached out not only to the crippled and mourning but even to the unjust, yet wealthy, tax collector. He makes it clear that there is something worthwhile in everyone, no matter what one's social status, reputation or standard of living. At that time this awareness wasn't really new to us, but just happened to strike us in a new, more profound way—thanks to the Holy Spirit.

The need to reach out more directly to the materially poor began to grow in our hearts as a couple. Granted, there are all kinds of, and ways of, being "poor." But to us the materially poor seem to suffer more because part of their poverty is the fact that they do not usually respond socially in a way that is "acceptable" to most; seldom are they able to do anything about the injustice done to them.

They don't have the power that money provides that can often help alleviate or lessen other types of poverty. The pain of immobility, another poverty they experience, is something most of us can't even comprehend.

Without trying to justify it any further, let us simply say that we had experienced a strong urging in our prayer, and in our sharing with each other, to take concrete steps in our lives to open up ways of ministry with the materially poor. It was difficult for us, as it is with most people, to begin making a new move unless we are fairly confident of what is going to take place, and how it is going to turn out.

Widsom certainly cannot be thrown to the wind. Jesus did tell us to make sure we have the necessary raw material before we start to build (Lk 14:28). Yet we sometimes think we need more raw material than is really necessary, and this can become a good excuse for inaction.

As a family we began slowly, wanting to allow the Lord to speak to us, one way or another, about what we were experiencing in our hearts. Our family prayer times included many moments of sharing the needs of others, particularly children who suffer famine, war and other types of poverty. This practice was a small but important building block to which our children responded, each in his or her own unique way, by expressing compassion for those in need.

A few years later we took a "mission" bus trip with our three children, and some people from the community of which we were a part, from New York City to the Texas border (fifty-six hours). We spent Christmas time working with a group who minister to the very poor in the "colonias" (poor neighborhoods) of a Mexican city just across the border.

The joy we experienced there of being with those people, sharing their pain with them, praying together, working and suffering with them, served to strengthen the conviction in our hearts of wanting to serve, through the church, with the poor. We knew that any way we would serve with the poor would have to do primarily with sharing the love of Jesus and trying to draw and encourage in them a personal response to his love. This ministry would of course have to be in the context of a concern for their material well-being as well. We became so convinced that the freedom and peace that can really affect their lives in a lasting way, as it has ours, can come only from an awareness of the personal love of Jesus for them.

It is still quite difficult for lay people, particularly couples and families, who discern a call to total service in the church, to find a way to do that. There seem to be so few patterns or paths. In our own case, we saw that the next step that would be important for us would be to study Spanish. A growing percent of Catholics in the United States are Hispanic in background and often in language. The materially poor Hispanic person is often Catholic. This catalyzed our going to Texas (with the discernment of our community) to study pastoral Spanish and missiology, through a grant we received from a missionary community.

During this time of our mission internship in the southwest, reflection on the mystery of Christ's experience of abandonment on the cross (Mk 15:34) became very significant for us. A major change occurred in the community of which we were a part, and we experienced a very painful severance from Christian brothers and sisters to whom we were committed for a number of years. The effect was to pull the foundation for our service from under us. All of a sudden we were alone, by ourselves, and seemingly exiled. This was a tremendous struggle for us. What we experienced is that in the process of trying to be open and prepared for ministry with the poor, we became one "with" them, one "of" them, in ways we never would have chosen or imagined would happen. Where community had always been very foundational in our following Jesus, all of a sudden we were painfully without it. So, with the Lord's grace, the challenge was to thank him and affirm the fact that he had not abandoned us, no matter how we felt. We also experienced material poverty at that time, since our stipend ended also. The Spirit inspired a Franciscan missionary priest to send us his retreat stipends. Also our good friend, Catherine Doherty (founder of Madonna House Apostolate), herself in a ministry with the poor, very kindly helped us during those very difficult months. She said to us: "We're the poor, helping the poor."

At this time of want, we became more spiritually connected to the Blessed Mother, especially through our so frequently seeing her imprint on plaques and pictures honored everywhere on walls in Mexico and Texas, as she had appeared to Juan Diego in the sixteenth century, and is known as Our Lady of Guadalupe. We became ever more conscious of Mary's place in the church and in our lives, especially as we had experienced the poverty of being without community. We felt so poor, so conscious of how the pearl of true identity as brothers and sisters in Christ seemed to slip through a crack in the community heart and rolled under the consciousness of the members. Consequently, we were becoming quite sensitized to the meaning of "being poor."

In our prayer, especially asking Mary's intercession, we became focused on her image on the tilma of Juan Diego. We knew that for the Mexican Indians of the sixteenth century, the moon was a symbol of one's true reflection, and since in the image Mary is standing on (a "crushing" symbol) a black moon—a false reflection—she is crushing the false identity the Mexicans had of themselves, i.e. as an inferior people, without identity.

We thought: Mary, who knows her own identity as the immaculate conception, crushing the serpent of evil, and as co-redemptrix (with Jesus), is winning the victory: that we might know we are each and all God's children—our true identity; that we, in our poverty, may know our wealth, our rich inheritance as sons and daughters of our Father and brothers and sisters of Jesus; and that nothing can separate us from his love (Rom 8:35). We are, therefore, all brothers and sisters to one another.

Francis of Assisi is a model we looked to in understanding that involuntary poverty, i.e. not knowing "who we are," is an evil. We've come to see that this is the most devastating poverty. Yet to identify with our brothers and sisters because of Jesus himself becoming poor, becoming one of us, gives positive redemptive meaning to chosen poverty. Jesus' mission was anointed by his Spirit, "sent to bring good news to the poor" (Lk 4:18), good news about who they really are. In this profound mission, and by his grace the last ten years, we have been privileged to share.

After spending some months studying the Spanish language and culture we discerned through prayer and spiritual direction to stay in Texas for a year and work as "lay ministers of evangelization" in a materially poor, Mexican–American parish. This experience was very fruitful for us and served to strengthen the conviction in our hearts to commit ourselves to evangelizing with the poor. It has become an advantage and privilege for us to know that we are indeed one of them, in deep need of the "good news."

From this experience emerged LAMP (Lay Apostolic Ministries *with* the Poor), a service community that shares in that mission of Jesus: "The Spirit of the Lord is upon me because he has chosen me to bring the good news to the poor . . ." (Lk 4:18). The scripture also tells us to let our light shine and not to hide this lamp (see Lk 8:16).

In this book we share his light through experiences of some of the LAMP ministers and their efforts to respond to the challenge of the gospel. In many ways it is a matter of taking the risk to see the needy around us and to reach out to them—not because we have something to "give" them, as much as our wanting to be "*with*" them, and together discovering Jesus in the human condition of our brothers and sisters.

Even though this missionary service, at this writing, is in this country, it frequently carries with it all the challenges of a foreign missionary response. Far from simply being a recounting of experiences, the purpose of this book is to encourage, to motivate, to inspire the reader to respond to this same gospel mandate in each of our unique situations. There is no need for any of us to say: "If only I were in that situation, then I could do something."

Although we are advocates for supporting social action on their behalf and help to provide food, clothing and other physical needs they may have, the main way we seek to serve through LAMP is by being a faith-supporting presence with the poor. Certainly their physical needs can be enormous, but their inner life is often starving for a deeper awareness of their identity through the Lord's love.

LAMP ministers will share how, through their everyday service and sometimes unknown to them, someone was deeply touched and experienced a healing in their relationship not only with God but also with the church. We all know people who have stopped participating in the faith community for numerous reasons. Usually these reasons had to do with a deep hurt they experienced, possibly many years before. But when they encounter people, who for them represent the church, reaching out to them with unconditional love, that becomes a healing and reconciling experience for them. As LAMP ministers, there is nothing that gives us greater joy than to see someone return to being a participant in the Christian community through this ministry. We feel it is a miracle of God's grace to be channels in which someone's heart is changed that radically. Surely St. Michael and guardian angels significantly share in that role.

At the other end of the spectrum is the miracle of faithfulness. How it builds all our faith to be with someone who has, through difficult and trying experiences, remained faithful and active in their service of the kingdom! Such a person is our associate director, Marybeth Greene. Her faithful following of the Lord has deeply affected our family. She made a radical commitment to follow Jesus on a retreat weekend in 1967, and has been steadfast and faithful ever since, through very challenging times. That weekend has become known as the "Duquesne Weekend" and is considered to be the beginning of the Catholic charismatic renewal. The loving presence and service of Marybeth has greatly affected the development of LAMP. She also has a particular gift in drawing children and youths into a meaningful relationship with Jesus and an awareness of the poor. Her service as director of Lamplighters has been profoundly fruitful and life-changing for those who have been a part of it. (The accounts in this text relating to youth were coordinated by Marybeth.)

Throughout this past decade and continuing is the faithful intercession of the communion of saints, our per-

manent community on our mission. We ask those who
have gone before us, marked with the sign of faith, to intercede for us on this challenging journey.

Tom & Lyn Scheuring
Feast of the Holy Family, 1991

Foundations

THE BEGINNINGS OF LAMP
Tom & Lyn Scheuring

On March 25, 1981 (Feast of the Annunciation), we received a letter from Cardinal Cooke (the archbishop of New York at that time) in response to our proposal to begin a lay ministry of evangelization with the materially poor in the New York area. He responded affirmatively and invited us to begin researching its feasibility. Later we also met with Bishop Mugavero of Brooklyn and Archbishop Gerety of Newark and received their blessing to begin LAMP in their dioceses.

At our seventh anniversary, Cardinal O'Connor spoke about LAMP and in particular focused on the word "with" in the official title of this ministry: "Lay Apostolic Ministries 'With' the Poor." He saw that word, which we chose very carefully at the beginning of this ministry, as significant in describing the posture we are all to have in our service of others, that is, a relationship of equality rather than giving "to" the poor or doing things "for" the poor.

In chapter eight of the major life of Francis of Assisi by St. Bonaventure, there is a description of Francis' attitude toward the poor which greatly inspires us:

> He responded with a remarkably tender compassion to those suffering from any bodily affliction. He had an inborn kindness which was doubled by the kindness of Christ infused in him from above. Therefore his

15

soul melted at the sight of the poor and infirm, and to those to whom he could not extend a helping hand he extended his affection. Once it happened that one of the friars responded gruffly to a beggar who had asked for an alms at an inconvenient time. When the devoted lover of the poor heard this, he ordered the friar to strip himself, cast himself at the beggar's feet, confess his guilt and beg for his prayers and forgiveness. When he had done this humbly, he added: "When you see a poor man, my brother, an image of the Lord and his poor mother is being placed before you. Likewise in the case of the sick, consider the physical weakness which the Lord took upon himself." That most Christian pauper saw Christ's image in all the poor; and when he met them, he not only generously gave them even the necessities of life that had been given to him, but he believed that these should be given them as if theirs by right.

Non-voluntary poverty isn't to be glamorized. It is the result of selfishness, of sin in the world. The persons who are the victims of this situation, often for generations and centuries, are the closest we can get to the victimization that Jesus experienced on earth. It is to these, who experience so keenly the effects of sin in society, that we are to give a "preferential" concern. The church speaks of it as a "preferential option for the poor." (One among many references to this option from ecclesiastical sources is an "Address to Curia and Cardinals" by Pope John Paul II in January 1985.) In no way is this meant to ignore those who are poor in other ways, but rather to show a particular concern for those who lack the basic necessities of life.

What each LAMP minister discovers in our ministry "with" the poor is that we, i.e. the LAMP ministers, are really the ones who are being evangelized, who are being confronted with God, with the love of Jesus, with our own sinfulness, in ways we never expected.

The poor evangelize us! Now how could that be? We are the ones who are trained, who have gone through the formation, who are "qualified" to serve in a ministry of evangelization. How could the poor evangelize us?

Before that question is addressed, may we say a word about "evangelization" itself? In 1975 Pope Paul VI wrote a document, an Apostolic Exhortation to be exact, entitled: "On Evangelization in the Modern World." A number of very interesting things were written in that document. One of the strongest statements of the document is: ". . . the task of evangelizing all people constitutes *the essential mission of the church*" (n. 14). In that same paragraph, Pope Paul states: "Evangelizing is in fact the grace and vocation proper to the church, *her deepest identity. She exists in order to evangelize . . .*" In wanting to understand more deeply just what evangelization is, we read: "For the church, evangelizing means bringing the good news into all the strata of humanity from within and making it new" (n. 18).

Initiating a pioneer ministry such as LAMP was challenging for us, and only by the grace of the Holy Spirit could we as lay persons begin a type of ministry that usually came from a religious community: needing to raise all the funds ourselves; connecting appropriately with the church in unity with the hierarchy—which was and continues to be of utmost importance to us; recruiting people for such a new type of ministry where they would be willing to share their faith and pray with people. Our motivation came from our commitment to the Lord (by his grace), especially through our baptismal call and our desire to serve, through the church, with the poor through evangelization.

Shortly after founding LAMP Ministries, we were approached by a religious community who invited us to make LAMP their "lay" outreach. This community would subsidize LAMP, assist its spreading, recruitment, keep the books, etc. This kind of security and assistance was very appealing, considering our recent past. Let us explain. After returning from missionary work in Texas, we were unable to afford rent for an apartment in New York City. It was on the feast of St. Joseph that a Bronx man, who helped missionaries, offered our family of five a small apartment which was set up for missionaries. We were so grateful for the Lord's providence. Coupled with the responsibility of parenting our children and helping them adjust to a move into a large city and all that entails, and feeling the great financial pressure of raising a family, the security of the religious community's offer was extremely enticing to us.

The vision we perceived the Spirit giving us for LAMP, however, persisted. We couldn't embrace that attraction of material security if it might compromise what the Spirit seemed to be saying to us at the time—that somehow it was very important for there to be witnesses of this kind of lay initiative in the church: of lay persons, drawing on their baptismal responsibility, to participate in the mission of the church, and serving in "clear" unity with the church. We had had contact with single and married Christians of other denominations who followed the Lord into active ministry with uncompromising commitment. Couldn't that become more possible in the Catholic Church?

Our book *Two for Joy* (on married spirituality) began with the gospel parable of the king who had a banquet and invited many. The response of one invited guest was "no" because he said, "I have married a wife, and therefore I cannot come" (Lk 14:20). The man's marriage became an excuse for him not to respond to the invitation. We not only believe marriage is not an obstacle to many forms of non-ordained ministry, but through our efforts and struggles, we hope we have given witness to some of the possibilities that do exist—that all are called to respond to the gospel in some way.

And so we have continued since then, sometimes feeling quite isolated as a family, except for our associate director Marybeth. Isolation is particularly experienced because of the usual temporary nature of the LAMP ministers' commitment, that is, people coming for a year, two or three and then leaving. Saying "goodbyes" and continually starting over with new people motivates us to see our call in the context of the larger church, a "school of evangelization," teaching people who will benefit the church wherever they go. Knowing that once LAMP ministers have experienced their hearts being stretched in compassion for and with the poor and formed in a ministry of evangelization, they and those they affect will become deeply committed to the kingdom of Christ.

Perhaps this experience is common in all volunteer groups, but because we have seen the importance for us and our children to be supported in a Christian milieu in a more stable way, it is often a struggle experiencing the transiency of those committed Christians who serve with us for a short time. Even though there are many people who encourage us, such as Marybeth and Ed Greene (a LAMP minister who has been with us almost from the beginning), when we really need it, the permanent relationship with the Lord in daily eucharist and our prayer life is our main sustaining community through every joy and every sorrow. The Poor Clare Monastery in the neighborhood has been our daily place for eucharist and prayer.

The abbess, Sr. Elizabeth Enoch O.S.C., and the sisters have been an encouraging light through these years; as well as Fr. Andre Cirino, O.F.M., and other Franciscan brothers and sisters.

Integral to the grace of our love for the church and our vision for LAMP is the fact that lay single and married couples, as well as religious sisters, share a common commitment as LAMP ministers, benefiting from the ongoing support and formation that is provided in LAMP. Religious, lay and clergy serving together is central to LAMP's ecclesiology—"completing" each other, not "competing" with each other.

The responsibility for directing a school of formation motivated us to take courses to reinforce our knowledge of theology. We saw the importance of more firmly grounding our teaching of the LAMP ministers in a solid foundation of church history, Catholic ecclesiology, scripture, doctrine, the social teachings of the church, etc. Financial providence specifically for these studies enabled us, over a number of years to take a course at a time, to receive our Ph.D. degrees in theology. Our dissertations were also in areas pertinent to the areas of formation in LAMP. Lyn had as her subject "The Poverty of Francis of Assisi According to Bonaventure and Its Relation to Poverty in John of the Cross." Tom's topic was " 'Evangelii nuntiandi' and the Puebla 'Final Document': Their Effects on the Mission of Evangelization with the Poor."

In 1986 we undertook another challenge through LAMP. We expanded this evangelistic ministry into full-time service in welfare hotels for homeless families in New York City. These are hotels, some in midtown Manhattan, which the city welfare department rented in order to house homeless families. There were no patterns for this kind of ministry. It required struggling through New

York City agencies to get permission for our presence and for some space for a desk in these hotels. The doors seemed to close at first because those in charge of the hotels and agencies working there couldn't see the value of such a service. There were many temptations for us to feel discouraged and disheartened, wondering if we were dreaming the impossible. But we came together with other LAMP ministers and prayed for the Spirit to open the doors through Mary's intercession, truly believing that she, mother of the church, would want a clear witness of the Lord's presence, through the church, to her poor, disenfranchised, homeless children in the shelters where there is such confusion and disintegrated family values. Within a few hours after these prayers, we received a call from those responsible, saying that a LAMP minister would be allowed in the hotel in a capacity they could refer to as a "receptionist." This brought great joy because it enabled the LAMP minister to be more visible and available than we had ever expected. After all, a receptionist is one who "receives" others (in the name of the Lord). It was perfect—truly a victory for the Lord.

This new outreach was also a financial challenge for LAMP, because there was no parish to provide room/board, medical insurance and a stipend for the LAMP ministers serving in this way. But we believed that it was God's will and "his" service, and that these families (five hundred in one hotel, including about fourteen hundred children) deserved a daily presence of the church and a faith-supporting ministry.

LAMP ministers seek to be communicators of the good news through our caring, our listening, our words and our actions, basically through our "being with . . ." Nonetheless, we are so often the ones on the receiving end. We hear expressions of faith and trust from those who have so very little. This causes us to reflect on the lack of depth in our own faith. We see the forgiving spirit of others that causes us to repent for not loving more readily. It can take many forms. We'll share an example.

One day a LAMP minister, serving in a welfare hotel for homeless families, was talking with a mother. This particular mother had been very upset because one of her little children had had an accident and was in the hospital, though not in serious condition. The LAMP minister was speaking with her and trying to console her. She suggested that the two of them take a walk over to the church and ask God for help. The mother declined, however, saying that she didn't think she could go with her. After asking again, and again being denied, the LAMP minister asked the mother if she was Christian. With lowered head, the mother's soft but clear voice responded: "Sometimes!" Her response was a challenge for us to be aware that our so glibly saying we are "Christian" may mean we don't truly realize that it is not a label or an organization we belong to, but the way we live our lives, and that perhaps we are not Christian at "all times." How can that not cause us to stop and think? As we are reading this, perhaps we can take a little time and allow the Spirit to speak to our hearts through that homeless mother.

It builds the faith of all of us to see the changed hearts and lives because of the Spirit's work of love through a LAMP minister. We are seeing the healing power of a loving presence accompanying the direct sharing of the gospel message. This is the service of a LAMP minister— to share the gospel while communicating God's care through a loving presence. "The harvest is great but the laborers are few" (Lk 10:2). The masses of people in the inner city, needing to be reached out to, are an overwhelming challenge to a pastor and staff. "You are my lamp, O Lord! O my God, you brighten the darkness about me" (2 Sam 22:29). Looking to this lamp, who is the Lord, LAMP ministers are helping meet this challenge.

The witnesses in this book, however, can be very misleading. It can make this ministry seem so glorious, easy, and always successful. This isn't the case. Loneliness, disappointing results, failed attempts, confronting one's own sinfulness—such is also part of a missionary's call and something we also experience as we pick up the cross and follow Jesus. The drama and excitement of the mission carries a LAMP minister through the difficult moments of the first few months, but that soon wears away, and commitment to the Lord and loving his people, no matter what, has to take over as the sole reason for undertaking such a challenging ministry.

> For God, who said, "Let light shine out of darkness," has shone in our hearts, that we in turn might make known the glory of God shining on the face of Christ. This treasure we possess in earthen vessels, to make it clear that its surpassing power comes from God and not from us (2 Cor 4:6-8).

As LAMP is considered a "school of evangelization," every Monday we meet together with the other LAMP ministers for a time of teaching, sharing experiences of the previous week, praying together, supporting one another, and studying in particular the gospel of Luke or papal documents such as *Evangelization in the Modern World,* applying what we discuss to our own situations of ministry with the materially poor.

What we have seen consistently grow within all of us, as we spend this time reflecting and sharing, is a deepening awareness of the gift the poor are to us. Their faith nurtures ours, their simplicity disarms us, their vulnerability challenges us, their love feeds us. This ministry isn't the great thing we are "doing for them"; rather it is the very door through which we are finding Jesus in our own personal poverty.

As church, we need the poor, the gift they are as human beings and as our brothers and sisters in Jesus. We all have many fears that would keep us from opening our hearts and lives to them. Jesus was very consistent, however, in what he said on those occasions when people were being challenged to a major leap in their faith: "Be not afraid" (especially in Matthew 14:28—Peter being called to walk on the water). His word strengthens: "Your word is a lamp to my feet, a light on my path . . ." (Ps 119:105).

In times of fear and doubt we struggle to have those moments, through the Spirit's help, be opportunities to grow in trust. It is never easy in such a challenging ministry, but the dedicated service of the LAMP ministers makes it all worthwhile.

Following the next section, in which Marybeth shares the story of her call, this book continues as a journal of ministry with the poor. It is about a journey which each in his or her own way is called to enter, because each of us is called to share in the mission of Jesus.

A MISSIONARY CALL
TO FAITH AND TRUST
Marybeth Greene

When Tom and Lyn first wrote a description of what was to become LAMP Ministries, they sent me (and many others) a copy for my prayer and reflections. Reading it over, I was immediately drawn to its mission. For several years I had been experiencing a great desire to discover more deeply the person of Jesus by being in ministry with the poor. This had led me to work for an office of several black inner-city agencies (day care, housing, abused children and women), during which time I was privileged to work side by side with many African-Americans, learning much about their culture and their past and present suffering. I also spent a summer teaching in a CYO camp for inner-city children. Grateful for these opportunities, yet hungry for a more direct ministry role, I began to work as a campus minister at Manhattan College. Each of these jobs had elements which were part of what I was drawn to, yet none had all the elements together: ministry, youth, the poor.

To explain how these came to be my attractions, I would have to point to several experiences of God in my life, who has called me by name to follow in the footsteps of Jesus. Twenty-five years ago, when I was a student at Duquesne University, my life was forever changed by the action of God—Father, Son, and Spirit—during a weekend which became known as the start of the charismatic renewal in the Catholic Church.

I had been part of the faculty–student group which planned the weekend, centered around the beginning chapters of the Acts of the Apostles, and a book called *The Cross and the Switchblade* by Rev. David Wilkerson. Little did I know how God wanted to use those readings and that weekend to bring me to a (young adult) conversion to Jesus and an overflowing of the Holy Spirit in my life, and, even more incredibly, to touch many thousands, even millions, of lives around the world with his personal love and power to serve.

This weekend came at a time in my life when I was searching for meaning. My childhood experience of God had been pure and simple and happy, complete with joyous faith-filled memories of first communion, May crownings, singing in the children's choir at daily mass. These are some of the moments which had rooted my life in God and the church.

During my freshman year in college, the Christian group to which I belonged spent an evening during Christmas vacation at a "house of hospitality," a Christian center for men who lived on the streets of the Hill District in Pittsburgh. This experience, especially, profoundly affected my relationship with God, and caused me to question how I could continue to live such a relatively easy life when so many others had lives full of suffering and disappointment.

By the time I was a junior in college at Duquesne, I was looking for a deeper conviction of God. During my high school years, my family had moved from the little mining town where we had lived to Pittsburgh, and the transition to city life was not easy for me or for my family. Moreover, my studies in history, theology and psychology were stretching my mind, and also shaking my simple faith. How did I know if God was real? Seeing some things in the church which I could not reconcile with the gospel, abuses concerning money and power, left me with questions.

Reading *The Cross and the Switchblade* before the weekend, I was very touched by God's love for the young people who were in gangs on the streets of New York. God touched their lives deeply, which moved me to tears as I read their stories. Before the weekend, I knelt by the side of my bed, and for the first time in many months I prayed from my heart, saying, "God, if you are real, I want to know. I won't fight you anymore, but want for my life what you want from now on." That was the opening which allowed God to show me his presence and love.

It was at the celebration of the eucharist the Saturday of the weekend that conversion took place. At the sign of peace before communion, I was aware of the presence of Jesus among us, and I was afraid suddenly of giving my life over to him. This hesitation stayed with me as I greeted my friends, nodding to them as they expressed the peace of Christ to me. I didn't want to say anything, because I intuitively knew that verbalizing the peace of Christ to others meant that I believed and committed my life to Jesus without reserve, which scared me! It was when I greeted one of the professors there that my fear was overcome. When I nodded to him as he offered the peace of Christ to me, he said emphatically, "Say it! Go on! You can say it!" "The peace of Christ," I responded back to him, and the floodgates of grace seemed to break open, making the presence of Jesus within me, among us, and in the eucharist tangible and very real. After receiving the Lord's body and blood, I began to weep with joy. When mass was over, my friends came to me, concerned. "What's wrong?" they asked. I assured them, "It isn't what's wrong. It's what's right!" The professor came over and offered his handkerchief, saying loudly, "Happy birthday!" He understood somehow the action of God in my heart.

That evening many of us present were drawn to the chapel before the Blessed Sacrament. As I entered the room, I could experience the presence of the Holy Spirit filling the chapel. It was like being immersed in water and light. We stayed in that place, spontaneously praying and praising the Lord for many hours that night. Much of our prayer was also intercession for the whole church, and for our bishop, and for those most in need of the Lord. It was a very familial time, and I knew God then as a family of Father, Son, and Spirit. We were caught up in that reality in a timeless way, caught up in being church. With this experience, my life's direction was solidified. Serving God and the church became the meaning for which I had been looking.

Several years later, I met Tom and Lyn at a house of prayer. I was very impressed by them, by their inclusiveness and openness as well as by their gift of discernment. That was over twenty years ago. The following year, they with their new daughter Maria, another lay person, a number of sisters and priests, and I lived in another house of prayer. During this time, many religious as well as lay people, and especially missionaries, came to stay for various lengths of time to enter into the prayer life there. It was a year with many blessings, which ended abruptly when the house went up in flames one May morning.

With no possessions except what was given me by many loving Christians, I went to live in a Catholic charismatic community, which for eight years was where God spoke to me and continued to form me and called me to serve. It was a great consolation for me that Tom and Lyn and their family were also called to serve there, and were in a primary leadership role.

Three very simple but far-reaching experiences stand out in my mind during that time. The first was an inner sense that came to me one day while I was in a library. I was writing something about children, and it came to me, I believe from the Holy Spirit, that loving children, treating them with respect and mutuality, was a door to loving the poor, the crippled, the lame.

Another key experience was a prophetic word given (by Lyn) at a powerful charismatic conference in Atlantic City. "Do you recognize me," the Lord asked, "in the disfigured faces of your brothers and sisters who suffer?" That question became a consistent part of my life, and gave shape to what the Spirit was unfolding within me.

Around the same time, while relaxing on a beach one day, I believe the Lord spoke one word to me: "Missionary." It gave me much freedom and joy to realize that my call was a missionary one.

Within a few years, the community which I loved and served seemingly changed its priorities of service, and a rupture took place. The suffering and rejection was multifaceted. It was a time pointing to the suffering and rejection of Jesus, whose yes to the Father through the desolation of the cross gives our own suffering worth and the promise of redemption.

However, the end result was that, just as nine years earlier, I had gone to that community with no material possessions because of the fire, I left with almost no material or communal supports. In many ways, I was poor. Others, in pastoral roles like mine, also left. My prayer is that the Lord will bring continual blessings to all who suffered through this experience.

It was in the year after this that Tom and Lyn sent me their proposal to begin LAMP. Right from the beginning I hoped that I could someday work with them in this new ministry of evangelization with the poor. When they returned to the New York area from Texas in 1981, I expected it would take a year or two before they could be ready to implement this service. In October I was very surprised to hear that the Spirit was paving the way to begin within a few months.

I was in a quandary. I wanted very much to be a part of LAMP, to be with and support Tom and Lyn in the very start of the ministry. However, the decision to actually leave a job with security, good salary (and four months of paid vacation a year) was not an easy choice to make. For a number of months after the community rupture, I couldn't find a job, and with no savings I really struggled to trust God each day. Working for the social agencies and then for the college was a relief from the financial and emotional strain of unemployment, and now it seemed God was calling me to step out in faith and trust for the sake of the poor. This was a time of deep soul-searching, repentance, and begging for God's mercy. Could I trust God? In the past it had been easier, but experiences of upheaval and disappointment had left their marks. Gingerly, but clearly, I discerned that this was God's will for me, a way to express the love he was nurturing in my heart for his poor.

Leaving campus ministry, I began to work part-time with LAMP, the other days seeking temporary jobs to pay bills and eat while we worked at creating a brochure, establishing channels for publicity, communicating with the ordinaries and pastors in the New York area, and various other things. For six months we shared a desk in a small Catholic gift shop with the store's bookkeeper, and with a friendly German shepherd who "lived" under the desk. The proceeds from this shop (a cluttered, unheated and poorly ventilated little room) went to support missionaries, and the owner offered the use of their desk because of LAMP's missionary focus. It was during this time, too, that Maria, Malissa, and Paul, with us, envisioned what has become Lamplighters. It is always a grace to remember beginnings.

What amazes me still, as I think of these years, are the LAMP ministers who have served or are serving, people who have come to us from many walks of life, from many parts of the country, expressing a call to share in the gospel experience of bringing and discovering the unconditional love of Jesus in the noisy streets, the crowded apartments, the forgotten single rooms of the city—where God's people live. Each LAMP minister has stories to tell. Each is a miracle of God's grace.

Perhaps the greatest joy for me is the relationship with the youth and children who want to grow in Christian compassion for those who suffer. These Lamplighters are integral to this ministry. I love to be with them when they gather, sharing and encouraging them to see themselves through the eyes of Jesus, each creative, unique and gifted, yet all together in unity expressing his love through their own love.

The senior Lamplighters (high school age) have noticed that when they speak to groups of adults and tell them about their trips to the Bowery to share food and conversation with the people on the streets, or their clown ministry at a school for the deaf, or their reflections on the "Children of War" (children from war-torn countries who tour the U.S. about every two years), the adults leave with tears in their eyes and smiles on their faces. The Lamplighters are amazed at how much spiritual power

and hope they seem to communicate through their expression of caring. In a world which sees youth often cast
in a negative light, we believe the words of Jesus who tells
us that the kingdom of God belongs to them.

In regard to youth, the words of Pope Paul VI express
our own concerns well:

> Their increasing number and growing presence in so-
> ciety and likewise the problems assailing them should
> awaken in everyone the desire to offer them with zeal
> and intelligence the gospel ideal as something to be
> known and lived (*Evangelii Nuntiandi*, 27).

We constantly pray to be a support to the young through
this ministry.

The cost of following Jesus, in the power of the Spirit,
to me seems to involve a constant struggle to rely on God
the Father's faithfulness as his call burns interiorly, impel-
ling me to be present with youth and with the poor, in
faith believing that my presence mirrors and (I hope)
magnifies God's presence. Even though circumstances are
unsure, and discouragement at times seems to creep too
close to my doorstep, I draw on the presence and prayers
of other Christians (those with us now and those who
have gone before us). With this support enabling me, the
reality of God's presence and heart of love is the ground
on which I seek to walk each day of my life.

> The city has no need of sun or moon, for its lamp is the
> Lamb . . .
>   Rev 22:5

GOD'S PRESENCE IN THE
POWERLESSNESS OF HIS PEOPLE
Kay Johnson

*Kay Johnson, a widow whose children are grown, was
the first LAMP minister who committed a year to sharing and living the good news with the materially poor.
Kay served at St. Augustine's in the South Bronx.*

I guess you could say it was restlessness I did not
understand that precipitated my serving through LAMP
Ministries. A very white middle class conviction that anyone who really tries can make it out of poverty kept me
bound and blind for many years of my life. I can only sur-
mise that the genuine love that was in my heart for Jesus
Christ kept him present in my life. That presence kept me
restless. Periodically I attempted to alleviate it, but the
framework I chose was too narrow. Constantly and fool-
ishly I tried to do something for God. Never did I give him
any space to do something for me. This past year, as a
LAMP minister in the inner city, he finally got his space.
Through the people at St. Augustine's in the South Bronx
he did make me more aware that our task is to become and
to leave the "doing" up to him.

I found myself asking: "How do our black brothers and sisters sing of being on the glory road?" Surely they have put their hands on their own "sacred" wounds, and when they reached into their sides they touched the heart of Jesus. They live with this mystery of God and of becoming.

In awe I witnessed faith, hope and charity become enfleshed in an elderly woman confined to her home by a crippling disease. The downstairs windows had been nailed shut by the police after she lost the sight of one eye following a beating by an intruder who robbed her of her radio, her iron, and a bag of groceries. She reminisced about the many years of joy she had had working for her church, her voice and her views still strong. "Who would have thought I'd end like this?" was a question she posed, full of wonder at the mystery, with no bitterness. She has only her God now and whomever he sends to her. This is clearly one of the personal experiences that speaks to me of the presence of God in the powerlessness of his people.

The spirits of despair, anger, resentment may dwell in many, but there dwells in a remnant "the spirit of love, joy, peace, patience, kindness, goodness, faithfulness, humility and self-control" (Gal 5:22). That is the spirit that will prevail. This past year as a LAMP minister God granted me the light of seeing those fruits of the Spirit in the bodies, souls and spirits of people who have witnessed for a long time the title "Christian."

FIELDS RIPE FOR HARVEST

The third week after he began his service of evangelization with the poor in east New York as a LAMP minister at St. Gabriel's Parish, Glenn Smith awoke one morning to find that the battery of his car was stolen. A young man from the parish, whom Glenn had begun to know, came by and expressed his indignation at the event. He also voiced a desire to see the perpetrators receive some rough treatment for their crime.

Glenn replied: "Well, Jesus says that we have to pray for our enemies, not harm them" (Mt 5:44). Amazed at this response, the young man said he didn't know Jesus said that. After a moment, he asked Glenn if he would teach him what else Jesus said.

OPPORTUNITIES

One week, while the pastor of St. Gertrude's (one of the poorest parishes in the Brooklyn diocese) was away, LAMP minister Frank Pavone received a call from a family whose father was dying. The person asked for a priest to come to see the father before he died. Frank told the person that the pastor was the only priest at that parish, and he was away for the week. Frank did tell them that he was a lay missionary, and he would be happy to come to visit the man, although he couldn't administer the sacraments. They were very grateful that anyone from the church could come.

Upon arriving at their apartment, Frank saw that the man was in the last stages of dying. He was, however, able to give some sign of entering into the prayer as Frank prayed for grace that the dying man would know God's personal love, for any reconciliation needed with God or others, and for a peaceful passing over to the next life. The man was still alive when Frank left, but died shortly after.

This encounter filled Frank with much gratitude to the Lord that as a LAMP minister he had the privilege of ministering to this man and his family at such a critical time.

Frank has often mentioned to us how happy he is to help out when the parish has its Bingo nights. He sees it as a great time to meet the people, to hear what is happening around the neighborhood, and to set up appointments to visit people when he can talk with them about their relationship with God. He has seen much fruit for the kingdom come from this very humble service of "bingo-assisting."

LAMPLIGHTERS
Marybeth Greene

Mindful that the call to share in Jesus' mission of bringing the good news to the poor is "from generation to generation" (Mary's words in the Magnificat), we began to hold gatherings for children which would reinforce their Christian faith and help them develop love and compassion—the good news of Jesus' own love—for the suffering poor. We named this club, and the children who come to it, Lamplighters.

When we are together, we stress to the children how much God's kingdom belongs to them, how special they are to God, and the privilege it is to be with them. People who have come to be with the children during the Lamplighter meetings, who have spent years educating children, tell us they are very impressed by how attentive and involved the children become during the gatherings. We think it is because their spirits are able to drink in something of God's kingdom, leaving them peaceful and able to enter into an expression of love for the poor.

Our first big venture for Lamplighters was a party for Halloween. Children dressed as saints in their home-made costumes, and we guessed each other's identities. During the afternoon the children were led to "Heaven's Gate" (the decorated basement of the LAMP Center) and then led into the "Throne Room" to meet a representative of Jesus. A "Cheer Rally" was a great success, with groups making up cheers to scripture passages. A prayer led by Fr. Peter encouraged the children to know they are the light of the world. Songs, games and snacks also helped make the day a festival of fun.

After this initial party, the children gathered monthly, and each time, in a relaxed and informal atmosphere, they participated and interacted through songs, prayer, films, games and creative projects which they make for the aged, the lonely, the homeless, and others who need a little sign of God's compassion.

Through arts and crafts, the children have made rosaries, the Mexican "Eye of God cross," and paper wall hangings, using their creativity to make these small gifts with Christian meaning to be given away by the LAMP ministers in the parishes where they are serving.

Over the summer the children gathered for four Friday afternoons in July. The theme developed was the death and resurrection of Jesus. Through clowning skits, done by Malissa Scheuring, Paul Scheuring, and Emily Bruno, as well as by Dave and Mel Henkelman, a Christian couple trained in clown ministry, the belief in the death and resurrection of Jesus was reinforced through symbols of nails, balloons, cocoons and butterflies. The thirty or so children were profoundly attentive as Dave put on his makeup and explained its symbolic meaning of dying to self in order to gain new life.

Another highlight of the summer occurred on the bank of the East River when the children, two by two, launched helium balloons on which were tied messages sharing the good news of God's love. Cheers and shouts simultaneously filled the air as balloons drifted up, danced crazily in the wind, and gradually disappeared from view.

Lamplighters is meant to provide Christian support for family life and a way for parents to support their children in deepening and enriching the Christian faith.

YOUTH EVANGELIZE THROUGH CLOWN MINISTRY

Another aspect of Lamplighters emerged when students of the local parish, preparing for confirmation, volunteered to serve with LAMP to fulfill their sacramental service requirements. Besides assisting in our office, they practiced clowning as a way of communicating the gospels, and visited the children at St. Joseph's School for the Deaf to reach out with their clowning. What a special time these children had together! Children from the two schools learned from each other (especially since verbal language is not needed for clowns), and as a result, some of the deaf children want to come to the Lamplighter meetings. What a gift to us!

These seventh graders also are leading a "Little Lamplighters" meeting, helping younger children, ages four to eight, to experience God's love and the importance of caring for others.

One mother, whose two daughters come to Lamplighters, told us that they love to be here because it's so peaceful when we gather. Our emphasis when the children gather every five weeks (between thirty and forty-five children each time) is to stress fun-filled and loving interaction. Competition and rivalry have no place in the Lord's kingdom, which *belongs* to the children, Jesus says (Mt 18:3). When children are free from the pressure to

41

compete, they respond with much openness and generosity of service.

THE HOMELESS

From the beginning of LAMP Ministries, we had a conviction that the Spirit wanted to open new avenues of service, in addition to poor parishes where LAMP ministers had already begun to serve. The only qualification was that LAMP was meant to be with the materially poor.

One afternoon during the first Orientation Week we had for new LAMP ministers, the group of us were praying and had just read from the scriptures the passage: " 'Lord, when did we see you hungry, or thirsty . . . naked . . . sick or in prison . . . ?' And the Lord will answer: 'Whatever you do to the least of these brothers of mine, you do to me' " (Mt 25:38–40).

Just then the phone rang, and when Lyn answered the call, the person on the other end asked: Would LAMP Ministries come and evangelize the homeless in Times Square? The caller was concerned about the homeless people. He wanted someone to serve full-time in a single room occupancy hotel where the homeless were living— people one step removed from the streets. Needless to say, God's word was graphically clear and evoked our "yes" to his poor.

We, Tom and Lyn, met with the concerned group of people and responded by sending LAMP minister Sr. Noemi Valdes, S.M.R. to be a presence among the people in a daily way, listening to them, sharing God's word with them. Ed Greene, another LAMP minister, started to spend Saturdays there, leading a faith-sharing group and visiting with the people. Sr. Noemi was at the shelter for a year and a half. Ed Greene has been going on Saturdays this past year, and here Ed describes his experience:

> I visit people in the lobby of the shelter, inviting them to a Bible study group each Saturday. There we read from the scriptures and reflect on the reading chosen. After this, we have coffee and snacks, spending time together. I usually then visit a particular elderly person, and go outside for a walk with her when she is feeling able.
>
> We often struggle with the question of God's justice. How can God be a just one by allowing evil and such poverty to exist? There is no easy answer, we find. We realize, however, that all evil stems from humanity's fallen nature. We are called by Christ to be loving persons, even to those at whose hands we suffer. We are empowered by the Holy Spirit to accomplish this and to bring about justice by peaceful means.
>
> This Bible study group serves as an outreach to members of the body of Christ who are often not welcome, not encouraged to attend other places of worship. It allows them to hear the gospel in terms they can understand.
>
> I'm at times asked for advice by persons who find themselves in extremely difficult circumstances. One woman, driven to prostitution because of hunger, asked for help on how she could escape from this trap which had victimized her. A man who would often take coffee and then leave stayed for the whole meeting one day and asked if he should go to a mental institution for counseling. Another man came to us, so distraught, even weeping because of his difficult situation, and we had the privilege to "weep with those who weep" (Rom 12:15).
>
> My faith in Jesus has been strengthened by my

evangelizing experience at the shelter. I meet him
in people so in need, yet who give so much. There's
Gladys, who sits on her milk crate, lame in both legs,
yet gives me a beautiful smile when I greet her, and
warmly asks me how I'm doing. Dorothy, though sick
herself, will ask how my family and friends are, and
offers her sincere prayers. Ray, Helen, Dan, Isabelle,
John, Bettye, Danielle, Theresa, Ed, Janice, Gina, and
Helen are my brothers and sisters in Jesus, who teach
me what faithfulness means.

THE POOR RESPOND AND EVANGELIZE

The Lamplighters received a special gift from Dorothy, who lives at the Times Square shelter. At their December meeting, the Lamplighters had made angel banners
which the LAMP ministers gave to people they have met in
their ministries, and Dorothy received one of these. She
was so pleased with the gift that she sent a sizable portion
of her own very limited budget to the children in appreciation. Needless to say, the children were deeply touched
by her total giving. Dorothy's generosity reminds us of the
scriptural story of the widow who from her want has given
what she could not afford, eliciting the quick approval of
Jesus (Lk 21:1-4).

WITNESSING GOD'S FAITHFUL LOVE

One cold, rainy day in October, LAMP minister Jim
Schaffhausen and Marybeth met Mr. Wilson. Jim visits a
large hospital as part of his evangelizing service at St.
Theresa's in Brooklyn, and that particular day Marybeth
was accompanying him.

Mr. Wilson had just had his larynx removed, and so could only communicate by using a note pad and pen. Jim asked the elderly gentleman if he would like to receive the eucharist. He printed with a shaky hand, "Everyday!" When asked if he would like the two LAMP ministers to pray with him, his face took on a stricken look as he motioned that he could no longer speak. Jim assured him that he didn't need to speak aloud to pray, and then Marybeth and Jim began to ask the Lord to fill Mr. Wilson with his peace as they gently laid hands on him. Tears began to run down his cheeks, and the Lord's presence and peace were evident. At that point, he pointed to a medal of Mary that Marybeth was wearing, so Jim promised that he would bring one for him. On sudden inspiration, Jim asked Mr. Wilson if he would like a rosary. His response was to throw up his hands in jubilation! Jim had obviously touched on a deep desire in his heart.

About two months later, Mr. Wilson died, but Jim had the privilege of visiting him often and praying with him just hours before his death. What a gift to be able to share faith with this brother in the Lord.

Two women, a mother and a daughter, whom LAMP minister Doris Struckhoff met in the neighborhood of Holy Spirit Parish in the Bronx, were alienated from the church. After initially sharing openly with Doris, they began to ignore her and not speak to her when they saw her on the street. As Doris prayed for wisdom about the situation, she felt the Lord leading her to write to them and ask them to forgive her if she hurt them in any way. Touched by her letter, they contacted her and invited her to visit them again. As a result, one of the women went to see the pastor about her marriage situation, and is presently planning to be married in the church.

Sr. Noemi, the LAMP minister who serves in the Times Square shelter, tells us of a woman who lives there, and she visits her quite often. Were it not for the shelter, this young woman (in her thirties) would be living on the streets. At times, because this woman is caught in financial, alcohol and prostitution problems, she is afraid to see Sr. Noemi because, as she describes herself, she is "bad." Yet she always comes back, because Sr. Noemi tells her over and over that God loves her, and even though he sometimes doesn't like what she does, he still understands and accepts her.

Glenn Smith, serving at St. Gabriel's in Brooklyn, shares this witness with us:

Pearl has been a member of the parish for twenty years. She served the parish in many different capacities during most of that time. When I first visited her, she was in a terrible way. Confined to her bed, her atrophied legs were in almost constant pain. Diabetes had severely limited her sight. Added to this were sleeplessness and a crushing sense of abandonment and loneliness. No one came to visit her anymore. The woman was in deep depression.

On my first visit, I talked with her for a while and I prayed with her. Before I left, I promised her that I would be back. For four months a group of parishioners and I have been praying with Pearl, and this has produced wonderful fruit, a miracle you might say. Pearl is a changed woman. The depression is gone. She sleeps eight hours a night, and the pain that plagued her is almost entirely gone. She even gets up and walks to the kitchen now, something which formerly would have been impossible.

Along with this, her relationship with God has

grown. She tells of her renewed prayer life. She listens to the Bible on cassette, and she is constantly praying for the parish. Needless to say, it has been a thrill and a privilege to be an instrument of the healing power of Jesus Christ.

Not only this, but just as important, the parishioners have experienced their own giftedness to a new depth. Seeing Pearl undergo transformation has strengthened their faith and affirmed them in their service to God.

A CALL WITH A DEEP SENSE OF JOY
Gladys Miranda, LAMP Minister

My life has been a continuous search in seeking to do God's will. Even as far as I can remember, my constant daily prayer has been: "Lord, use me, put me in a place where I can serve you." That silent prayer has continued to be a part of my daily communication with God.

I'd always been very active in my home parish, "Sagrado Corazon de Jesus," in Vineland, New Jersey. I had been active in C.C.D., parish council, prayer groups, etc. Because of the example and commitment of the priests of this parish, I began to experience a call to Christian service. I had a sense that there was something else God wanted me to do, and so there was a time of "waiting on the Lord," a time of searching.

It was during this time that I had an opportunity to attend a Leadership conference in Edison, New Jersey, in 1983. At this conference I first heard about LAMP and met its co-director, Tom Scheuring. Tom explained LAMP to me and handed me a brochure to take home, pray and discern. To this day I can still recall feeling a deep sense of joy and excitement over this new possibility. I discussed this with Fr. Al, my spiritual director, and after some dialogue and prayer, he said to me, "This sounds good. Look into it."

That was my beginning in LAMP, and on September 11, I began my evangelization ministry in St. Boniface Parish in downtown Jersey City. St. Boniface serves a large, vibrant Hispanic community, made up mostly of Puerto Ricans and Dominicans.

My main ministry here is going out among the people, visiting their homes, to instruct them on occasion, to be present to them, to affirm, encourage, and draw them into a deeper life with Jesus and the Christian community at St. Boniface.

For example, I went to visit a woman recently who had not been attending mass with the parish or participating in any other way. As I was able to share with her, she began to confide in me that she was not married in the church. I continued to visit and share with her, and she began coming to mass. It was such a joy for her to experience that she is loved and welcomed in the parish. All her family members now come with her. I am continuing to instruct her, and she now meets with the pastor who is helping her in her marriage situation.

Another privilege I have experienced is visiting a family whose ten year old son is suffering from cancer. It is an experience of being present with the love of Jesus to this family, praying for them, and in a special way affirming how present Jesus already is to this vulnerable family right now.

Fall 1984

THE LORD OPENING US
TO NEW POSSIBILITIES
Peter and Monique Moussot

Peter and Monique Moussot, a young, recently married couple, are LAMP ministers serving the Lamplighter youth. Here they share how they came to be part of the LAMP Ministries community.

Ever since we first gave our lives to Jesus, we desired to help others come into relation with the Lord. We knew that God had called us to each other as a team. We kept praying and asking the Lord to lead us to a community where we could experience the type of love and support which would enable us to go out "two by two" and proclaim the good news.

Quite by "accident" we came in contact with LAMP Ministries and our prayers were answered. Here was the opportunity for which we had asked. We found that it was possible to serve God while holding our secular jobs, being married and working in our own home parish.

Now as we work with LAMP the Lord is continually opening us up to new possibilities in our call to serve him. We have found the joy of proclaiming God's love and joy through clowning and mime. Also we are coming to experience God through visiting with the poor. It is enlightening for us to come to know the richness of Christ even in poverty. Our hearts are constantly being stretched to know and experience God as we minister to his children and teenagers. In fact since our involvement with LAMP and Lamplighters we are truly finding that it is in giving of ourselves that we receive.

LAMPLIGHTERS: GROWING IN SERVICE

Lamplighters gathered for the first time this school year for an All Hallows party (a Christian substitute for Halloween). Maria and Malissa and their friends Michelle, Maria, Marilyn, Jennifer and Karen formed a band called "The Glorifiers" which performed to the delight of the younger ones and the adults as well. Some of the boys from the Lamplighters clown ministry—Chris, Mike and Eddie—mimed a surprise clown skit, bringing smiles to everyone's face. Games and music, party food and a pumpkin hunt formed the backdrop for celebrating the saints as people who don't give up when they make mistakes, but always know they can turn to the Lord anew to receive his loving friendship. We try to make the games we play cooperative ones, so we can learn the way of peace by "disarming our hearts," in the words of the American bishops.

Some of the LAMP ministers brought children from their parishes to the party. Celeste told us that the three girls she brought said on the way home that they felt they were different because of all the love they experienced and the new friends they made, and because of what they learned about the saints. We were happy to hear that Jesus was experienced among us, and his Spirit is continuing to plant seeds of the kingdom through children coming together in love.

We see the Lamplighters who come regularly growing in a desire to serve. Nicky, a seventh grader, did all the leg work to help the clowns get ready, and volunteered to do many little tasks during the party. Three young girls, Jill, Valerie and Monica, asked if they could help clean up afterward. We are grateful to be able to be in the presence of these young friends of Jesus.

Sixteen Lamplighters went with Marybeth and Monique recently to hear young people from war-torn countries speak of their tragic experiences growing up in war, and of their commitment to peace. The "Children of War Tour" was an inspiring experience, urging us to work and pray for peace, beginning with our own attitudes and not stopping until the entire world can know peace.

Sr. Noemi Valdes, the LAMP minister among the homeless at a Times Square shelter, invited the Lamplighters clown ministry to celebrate the good news there the week before Thanksgiving. It was a joy for a group of teens, children and adults to mime gospel stories, especially communicating God's "preferential option for the poor" which the church is encouraging these days.

Sr. Noemi asked the Lamplighters to pray for one of the women at the shelter, Ruth, who is quite sick. Ruth had been a medical secretary at one time. However, her life drastically changed when she had a stroke not long ago. Ruth spent three months in a hospital recuperating, and during this time the room where she lived was rented to someone else. When Ruth left the hospital, she had no place to go but the streets. Eventually she made it into the shelter.

Through faithfully praying and sharing with her, Noemi is helping Ruth see the love of Jesus the Lord, who eagerly comes as "the sun of justice with its healing rays"

(Malachi 3:20). Please pray with us for Ruth and the many whose broken lives deeply need the healing presence of Jesus.

"KEEP US, O LORD, AS THE APPLE OF YOUR EYE" (Ps 17:8)

During a recreational trip, which either threatened or delivered rain every inch of the way, the LAMP Ministries community drove upstate one misty Monday in October to pick apples. Arriving at an apple orchard tucked in the mountains, we let out shouts of praise to God as the sun burst through the clouds at the exact moment we stepped out of the cars. We enjoyed a leisurely picnic lunch together, celebrating a birthday, and basked in the sunshine which we so much appreciated as a gift from the Father that day. Afterward we roamed through the orchards, climbing trees, jumping and stretching to pluck those shiny apples of many different varieties. Taste-testing was often in order, bringing us to acknowledge how delicious those fresh apples were.

Our day didn't end there, however. Climbing back into the cars, we drove south to Manhattan's lower East Side Bowery, where we spent some time sharing "the fruit of our labor" with the many who are forced to live on the streets there. We chatted with our homeless brothers and sisters as we moved slowly from street to street handing them the freshly picked apples. It was they who most often talked about the Lord. They welcomed us with their smiles of hospitality. Many seemed surprised that someone would not only notice them but would want to listen to what they have to say, and care enough to bring them apples they had just picked. This visit, with those we know the Lord regards as the "apple of his eye" (Ps 17:8), was very special to us. The apples were just a means to get closer to those who suffer homelessness. We ask God the Father to provide for their needs and protect them and we invite your prayers to join with ours.

BRINGING INTO THE LIGHT
A PEOPLE IN DARKNESS
Doris Struckhoff, LAMP Minister at
Holy Spirit Parish in the South Bronx

I was born and raised in rural Missouri. Little did I know that when I was twenty-five I would be working among the poor of the South Bronx in a Catholic parish evangelization ministry. Since my first experience of the Lord's personal love for me, I always knew that I wanted to serve the Lord, but the inner city was definitely off-limits to me. In 1983, when I was deciding what to do after graduation from Franciscan University of Steubenville (with a B.A. degree in theology), my first thought was to join a community and get a job teaching religion in a middle class neighborhood. I had gone to Philadelphia for an interview with the archdiocese there and had checked out a lay Christian community; I was pretty sure that's where I would be. However, as I spent time reading over my spiritual journals of a few years, I realized that threads of my relationship with God would seem to be fulfilled in an evangelistic ministry among the inner city poor. The Lord gave me a tremendous desire for this kind of ministry, so I came to New York to learn about LAMP and share about my desire. As we shared and prayed about it I experienced

God's call to serve through this ministry grow in my heart. After a time of prayer and discernment, I began serving as a LAMP minister at Holy Spirit Parish.

My first feeling upon entering the ministry was that I was not capable of sharing the good news with the poor. I knew absolutely nothing about what it meant to be poor in a big city like New York. But as the months have gone by and I have gotten to know and love the people here, I realized that this is truly a faith-filled people. Most times when I do home-visiting as part of the ministry, I spend most of my time just listening to them tell me their story of experiencing Jesus within their lives. My call is simply to uncover the light which is within these people: God's people. I have discovered God's love more through them than I have at any other time in my life.

Frances, a woman in her mid-sixties, is such an example of faith to me. Although she has heart problems and often is not feeling well, she always has a word of encouragement and has such a beautiful gift of joy. Last year as she was preparing for her baptism, she was a source of blessing for me so many times by her enthusiasm for full reception into the Catholic Church. She asks the Lord to heal her so that she can serve more fully at the parish here.

John, a young man in his mid-thirties, came to me one Sunday to discuss some of his problems in his relationship with God. As we talked, I realized that he had a need to forgive his father. I prayed with him for healing of his relationship with his father as well as for physical healing of his hand, which had been infected by a piece of glass stuck in it. Several days later, he came back and told me that he had gone to the hospital for an X-ray and there was nothing wrong with his hand anymore. His life has changed since that happened. He persevered through his struggles by the power of Jesus the Lord. It is very exciting to see him grow.

The parish as a whole is also growing in its ability and eagerness to spread the Lord's word in many different ways. I recently initiated a bi-lingual parish retreat, with seventy-five people from the parish attending. The exciting thing was that the people from the parish gave the retreat. When I asked Ralph, a young married man, to share his faith experience, his eyes lit up with excitement. He told me that he had been praying for some time that the Lord would open an avenue of service within the parish for him. My request was an answer to his prayers.

The young adult community within the parish is becoming involved in a clown ministry. It began last year as a response to a visit to Holy Spirit Parish from assistant director Marybeth Mutmansky and Peter and Monique Moussot of the Lamplighters clown ministry. Some parishioners who were present became excited with the thought and decided to put together a clown program at Christmas for the children in the C.C.D. program. I am directing this quickly growing ministry—something which I never thought would be possible for me. We come together about once a week to pray and share together about new ideas.

As a LAMP minister I am also using my musical gifts. I have sponsored an evangelization concert for the parish. I also work with the school children, teaching them music for school liturgies.

At the LAMP Center, there is a painting on the wall of light breaking through the darkness. I believe that painting sums up for me what the ministry is about. It means bringing into the light a people in darkness; in darkness as to who they really are (sons and daughters of God), and in darkness as to the gifts within them, gifts which are often not noticed by our complicated society. Through this ministry I am also finding out who I really am: a woman with gifts of service and one who stands constantly in need of God's love and care. One thing I know is that I would never have known so radically my own need for the Lord if I hadn't entered this ministry—and I am glad I know it!

Summer 1985

BEING CALLED TO HOLINESS BY THE POOR
**Sr. Nora Brick, O.F.S., LAMP Minister
at St. Pius V, South Bronx**

I am a Missionary Franciscan Sister. In the fall of 1983 I first heard of LAMP Ministries and was touched by its emphasis on an evangelistic outreach to the poor of New York, Brooklyn and Newark. My religious life has always been with the poor, starting in the South Bronx in 1950. In the days of segregation in the south I was blessed to be among those who suffer from this in Savannah, Georgia for sixteen years. Then I was with the Mexican and Haitian refugees in Florida who were the ones that brought the gospel message to me as no seminar or retreat has. The purely evangelistic approach of LAMP, I thought, should be another challenge for growth. "The poor have the gospel preached to them" is a frightful standard for any disciple to dare enter. Since Luke 4:18 is the gospel passage on which LAMP Ministries is based— "The Spirit of the Lord is upon me because he has chosen me to bring good news to the poor . . . sight to the blind . . . liberty to captives . . ." (Lk 4:18)—somehow I knew the poor would bring me to this growth.

I live in East Harlem and I work in St. Pius V Parish in the South Bronx, a distance of thirty-one blocks, which I walk each day. The ministry begins on the street. There are "hangout" areas along the way. "Sister, do you have a rosary?" "Sister, I need a healing," which is often a sincere confession of life's "slings and arrows."

Having gotten through that milieu, I arrive at St. Pius V on East 145th Street which brings the poem "The Wreck of the Hesperus" to mind. The church is the only building on the south side between Willis and Brooke Avenues. This street, victim of the ravages heaped on the South Bronx, is like many others in the area. I visit the homes of the parish, and Lincoln Hospital two days each week. The people here are mostly Hispanic or black. Some visits, either at home or in the hospital, are moments of real encounters with Jesus, where he has willed to release his healing love on us.

Maria, a patient at Lincoln Hospital, was in deep depression. Her right foot was to be amputated. She refused to consent to the operation and became suicidal. The hospital staff were concerned, and I was asked to visit her. We prayed together for her healing in body and spirit. The Lord saw fit to heal her and to restore circulation in her foot. Praise God, she is back home and full of joy and praise of God.

Last September, with the approval of my pastor, I started a charismatic prayer group. We meet on Tuesdays at 7:30 p.m. After six months the stirrings of evangelization can be felt and a desire to go out and spread the good news.

All the LAMP ministers support one another in prayer and in presence. We meet each Monday and have a teaching day once a month. The vision set before us is of the Lord, who inspired Tom and Lyn to enflesh it in LAMP Ministries. It is knowing the treasures that the poor bring to our church.

GETTING TO KNOW JESUS PERSONALLY

Joe Tysz has been serving as a LAMP minister since September 1984 in St. Rita's Parish, located in the very poor East New York section of Brooklyn. His work has primarily consisted of developing a home visitation program. Visits are mostly directed to people who have had their children baptized at St. Rita's. The vast majority of these people have little or no conception of a living knowledge of Jesus Christ as Lord of their lives. Witnessing to them about the joy and peace they can receive in getting to know Jesus in a personal way has been a key aspect Joe uses to evangelize this group. Praying with them and for their intentions has been a grace in helping their relationship with the church grow.

Joe visits other groups, too. He visits people who are on the parish mailing roster, who are mostly churchgoers, and people who have their children enrolled in St. Rita's School. Joe also has done outreach to the parents of the children who have already graduated from the school. Since St. Rita's School only goes up to the eighth grade, being concerned about the youth during their high school years is important, as many of them start moving from religious to public education.

Since the majority of people Joe visits are living on a subsistence income, they usually have many physical needs as well. Through the New York City needy food program Joe has helped develop a food pantry at the church, where he distributes food as part of home visitation. Clothing is also an essential need that people ask for, so distributing clothes is also part of his ministry. In trying to meet the physical needs of people, the door opens to evangelize, sharing about the Lord in a context where people experience a caring relationship.

Joe has been aware of the need for home visitations to continue after he leaves his ministry at St. Rita's. He is training the parishioners to do it. The parishioners who have accompanied him really enjoy the encounters they have. Their enthusiasm to share about the Lord has grown much since the beginning, and they are now recruiting others in the parish to reach out, making the Lord's presence in the parish community more tangible.

LAMPLIGHTERS TOUCH JESUS ON THE STREETS OF THE BOWERY

Some of the teenage Lamplighters asked if they could accompany adults from LAMP on one of the periodic visits we make to the Bowery (a destitute area of New York City). Taking several hundred sandwiches, colored Easter eggs, different kinds of fruit which friends donated, and scripture tracts, packed in individual lunches, we walked the streets on Holy Saturday, sharing food and conversation with our homeless brothers and sisters of Jesus. Reflections of the teenagers follow:

"When we were coming home, I felt that the poor were really rich and the average person like us is really poor. I said this because the poor people depend on each other for friendship and love, and the average people don't have to depend on each other because it seems we have material things to depend on. I believe this because if you don't have friendship and love, you are really poor. The most touching experience I had was when we were running out of food. I gave my last pack to a man, and another man was sitting right next to him. The man I gave the lunch to said, 'Don't worry, I'll share.' That man had nothing and he shared. That's what I mean when I say the poor are rich."

—*Matthew Hohl*

"When we arrived there most of us didn't know what to expect. We weren't sure who would respond to us and who would reject us. God protected us and we walked through the streets and talked with people. We felt as though we received a lot more than we gave to them. We felt as though God was talking to us through them. For me it was a wonderful experience."

—*Malissa Scheuring*

"Our trip was a very shocking time for me. On the way home we were discussing what we felt. I said I thought of it as a coin with two sides. We met people who were grateful for our care and some who said no. I felt this was really a good experience because it brightened up the rest of my day. I looked on things with more concern because I really saw how well-off we really are. Little stupid things that bother me are nothing compared to their problems of everyday life. I felt good about myself for being able to have the courage to do this."

—*Christopher Flood*

"Before the trip, I thought I would not be able to give food out to people living on the streets. When we started to give out the food I began to relax. One man said, 'I'll pray for you and you pray for me.' Others said, 'Peace be with you.' 'What you're doing is great,' and 'You don't have to worry—we're all brothers around here and we share.'

These responses are what touched me the most. They told me that even if you don't have much of anything, you can still have a great amount of love!"

—*Michael Keane*

" 'You made my day. Thanks!' and 'God bless you!' were just a few of the many responses of the homeless men living in the Bowery. Every few months my family and a few friends make lunches of sandwiches, cookies, colored or white hard-boiled eggs, and fruit to bring down to the Bowery. When we give these to the men, their entire faces light up and some begin conversations about life down in the Bowery, how they got there, or about the Bible! It's amazing to hear and see the faith of some of these men, even though they live the epitome of poverty. The men living there weren't born there, but found themselves trapped when they didn't pay a debt, or a close friend or relative died and they felt totally alone. It was amazing to see the unity among them, even though they came from many diverse backgrounds. I really appreciate going down there because it gives me a chance to do something for others, and makes me realize, even though I may doubt it at times, how fortunate I truly am."

—*Maria Scheuring*

Spring 1986

LAMPLIGHTERS CONTINUED: PROCLAIMING FREEDOM TO CAPTIVES

Lamplighters, the mission by and for children and youth integral to LAMP Ministries, continues to be a vehicle which allows them to grow in their Christian faith through compassion for those who suffer, and continues to inspire adults with their fresh insights and honest responses to the gospel.

Recently some of the senior Lamplighters (high school age) participated in a LAMP training session on youth ministry, and Matt Hohl shared this reflection: "I had a reputation for being a rowdy type, always acting out to get attention. I like to come to Lamplighters, because I can be myself here and not be afraid of being made fun of. I've been coming to Lamplighters now for three years. Here I'm respected for myself. Now I realize that I don't have to be a troublemaker to seek attention."

We have learned that the field where the homeless from New York City are buried is on an island not far from our Center. The men who bury them are prisoners in a special work detail. The Lamplighters wrote notes to the prisoners, thanking them for their service to those poor people who die nameless and alone. They also try to encourage these prisoners to believe in God's loving presence with them. We put these notes on a large poster, which Lyn and I (Marybeth) took with us to the island, at the invitation of a prison chaplain who invited us to come for a mass being celebrated there. While on our way to the island by police ferry, prison officials told us it was against the rules to bring anything on the island, but we could bring the poster for mass, providing we took it back with us.

During mass, the celebrant asked me to read some of the messages from the Lamplighters. As I read them, expressing concern and what a good friend Jesus is, the faces of these young men became very soft, moved by the fact that children would think to write to them. As soon as mass was over, they came to express their thanks: "Tell the children we are grateful!" All of them gathered around the poster to read all the notes.

At that point, the prison officials came to say they had changed their minds. They said they would like to keep the poster and hang it in the dining room so the men could read it when they liked.

Children and youth have a tremendous power to communicate the gospel and to bring about greater unity in many situations. Thank you, Lord, for giving your kingdom to little ones.

POWER IN THE NAME OF JESUS
Glenn Smith

Before I became a LAMP minister, one of the most tangible fears I had, was the fear of crime. During the time of discerning my call to LAMP Ministries, the Lord dealt with this area, increasing my trust in his love. Training for LAMP ministers includes emphasis on making prudent judgments and avoiding potentially dangerous situations.

For those situations not under control, all of us constantly pray for protection for one another.

Recently I had need to rely on those prayers. One Sunday night I was just about to get in my car and go on a home visit when the alarm in the parish Center sounded. This could have meant a burglary, but I assumed that it was a false alarm since this is a frequent occurrence at St. Gertrude's. Annoyed at this interruption in my schedule, I went into the rectory, got the keys, and went over to the Center to turn off the alarm.

After turning off the alarm, I scanned the big expanse of the hall with my flashlight, not expecting to see anything out of order. Instead I did discover that our stereo was on the floor, apparently taken from the Center's office. I immediately turned around and ran back to the rectory to phone the police, after which I returned to the Center. Only later did I remember that LAMP's training urged the ministers to never knowingly enter into such a potentially dangerous situation, especially alone.

I turned on all the lights and waited for the police to arrive, but I was shocked to see the burglar begin to climb through the window still open from his previous entrance. I ran to the nearest exit, fumbling through my bulky set of keys, praying that I could locate the key which opened that door. With the help of God I got the key in the door, but in the next instant he grabbed me. He was much bigger than I. Trapped in his bear hug, I cried out for mercy, pleading with him that he could have my money if he would just let me go.

My pleading had no effect, nor did my struggle to wrestle free of him. This man must have been desperate. In this state of fright and helplessness, with no police in sight and no sign of rescue, I cried out to the one who alone could save me.

"In the name of Jesus, let me go!" I gave the words as a command, shouting so that he would be sure to hear. In an instant, his hold on me was broken, and I was out of his grip and hurtling through the exit.

Safe in our neighbors' home, I caught my breath, praising the Lord and giving special thanks to him for the power of his name. During the following days, I continued in thanksgiving, vowing to be more prudent in the future and grateful for the protection of his name and for hearing our prayers.

MISSION POSSIBILITIES FOR MARRIED COUPLES

In the opening lines of Tom and Lyn's first book, *Two For Joy,* they quoted from Luke 14:16–20, where the man is inviting people to his banquet, but everyone had an excuse, even the people who said: "I have married a wife, and therefore I cannot come." His marriage was an excuse for him not to respond to the invitation. It is exciting to see that, far from being an obstacle, marriage provides a partner in service.

This summer sees two married couples beginning as LAMP ministers. Jennie Salgado, a married woman and also a registered nurse, is serving as a LAMP minister in the Bronx. In sharing her background, Jennie recalls: "For as long as I can remember I have been a Catholic. My parents didn't actively participate in the church but we were 'Catholic.' I spent the first eighteen years of my life away from the church. I married at age eighteen and spent another ten years away from it. In 1978 my life appeared to hit rock bottom physically, emotionally, and spiritually due to a series of negative circumstances. In my pain, anguish and despair I called out to God, begging him to have mercy on me. I prayed without ceasing until gradually in time I felt myself being immersed in the peace and love of God. I surrendered my life to Jesus Christ and began a new life. Within a year my husband Raul also gave his life to the Lord. The Spirit then led me to become a LAMP minister."

On one occasion, Jennie visited a sick person in the parish. For some reason, unknown to Jennie, this person had not been visited in months. Upon arriving she discovered the reason—he was a twenty-three year old man in the last stages of AIDS. He was in very much pain, reduced to skin and bones and given about three weeks to live. As Jennie was able to give her own fears to the Lord, she spent some time visiting with the man and his mother. Before leaving she prayed with him that his pain be relieved.

A few days later Jennie went back to visit him, accompanied by her husband Raul. The Lord had heard their prayer—the sick man said that his pain had subsided and that he was able to rest comfortably.

Neither the man nor his mother had been to church in years. Through the visits of Jennie and Raul with them, however, they both expressed a desire to return to church. Jennie arranged a visit by a priest and they both received the sacrament of reconciliation. The young man's love for the Lord has grown these last weeks to the point that he very much wants to attend church and tell people about the Lord's love. His weak physical state may not make that possible, but by sharing his witness here, we, as church, can give praise to God and our faith is strengthened.

He continues to struggle with the fear of dying, but has been helped very much by a picture of Jesus smiling, which Jennie put on the wall just next to his bed. In this picture Jesus is holding a lamb in his arms. Jennie told him that, when he experiences fear, he should picture himself as the lamb in Jesus' arms. What a cause to rejoice, to see God work with such power and compassion.

Glenn Smith and his wife Sherry also have begun serving together as LAMP ministers at Holy Rosary, a materially poor parish in Yonkers, a suburb of New York City. The pastor, Fr. Sexton, is very supportive of lay ministry and solidly encourages the service of evangelization provided by Glenn and Sherry in his parish.

Fall 1986

REVERSING THE EFFECTS OF VIOLENCE

Sr. Alice Fitzsimons, S.C., contacted us and asked if she might be a LAMP minister at St. Augustine's Parish in the South Bronx, where she had been serving for nine years in the school. Sr. Alice had known of the evangelizing work of LAMP because the very first LAMP minister had served at St. Augustine's and lived in the convent where Sr. Alice lived. While she knew she could do the same work on her own, she wanted the direction and community support which she knew LAMP provided.

Over the past year, Sr. Alice has systematically visited apartments and homes within the parish boundaries, going door to door to introduce herself and give information to the people about St. Augustine's services. If those she visits are open, she prays with them as well.

One family Sr. Alice has begun to visit regularly is the Caby family. Gene "Darryl" Caby was paralyzed from the chest down as a result of the notorious incident on the subway with Bernard Goetz shooting Darryl in the back. Through these visits, Sister Alice dialogues with Darryl, not coming to judgment about the incident, but making an effort to elicit faith and hope from the depths of his life. Sr. Alice perseveres in her visits, trusting that God is working through her to bring restoration and healing to his family and others like them "who wait in darkness and the shadow of death" (Lk 1:79).

It seems that Sr. Alice's loving and prayerful presence and care in this situation, undramatic as the results may at times appear, is actually reversing the effects of violence and through the power of the gospel beginning to bring about "the peace which the world cannot give" (Jn 14:27).

LIVES WHICH SPEAK OF DEDICATION

Frank and Trixie Knight were ready for a change in their lives after a few years of retirement in North Carolina. They were looking for a way to serve together in the church. While they expressed an interest in LAMP, and we explored some possibilities for placing a married couple in a poor parish, it wasn't until they wrote to their bishop, Most Rev. John F. Donoghue of Charlotte, and he wrote back to them suggesting they look into LAMP Ministries, that they were sure God was calling them to be LAMP ministers. Soon afterward a parish opened for them to serve in, and they were able to sell their home and move to New York.

Frank and Trixie are presently serving at St. Martin of Tours Parish in the Bushwick section of Brooklyn. At the direction of the pastor, focusing on evangelization through service, they are establishing in the parish a St. Vincent de Paul Society to meet the urgent needs of those suffering from spiritual, physical and financial loss.

They enjoy relating to the young people of the parish, and have worked closely with the recently graduated eighth graders in an extensive service program especially with the elderly poor.

Frank and Trixie have also developed and present a pre-Cana program, and are eliciting evangelistic leadership from married parishioners to continue to present this program over the coming year. They are using a couple to couple approach which they find very effective.

Their pastor, Fr. Dwyer, wrote of them, "Their lives speak of a dedication that is at once inspiring and challenging; their constant cheerfulness and 'can do' acceptance of any task adds more to the spirit of the parish than could ever be described or measured."

Summer 1987

HAPPY EXCHANGES

It has become a tradition for Lamplighters to visit St. Joseph's School for the Deaf each year. Our visit this spring was a happy exchange of gospel stories, insights, questions, and conversations. We feel right at home with these young people, so close to God's heart, who challenge us just by their responses to the challenges in their own lives.

This year, as a special gift for our friends at St. Joseph's, a number of the seventh graders learned to juggle! It's hard to say who enjoyed it more, those who watched or those who demonstrated the juggling. In the tradition of St. John Bosco, we hope that our juggling will make the gospel all the more attractive to the young.

"WE WANT TO BEAR FRUIT THROUGH PERSEVERANCE"
Joe Tysz

Joe Tysz, who married as a LAMP minister, now serves with his wife, Rosanne.

One of the aspects of being a LAMP minister, which my wife Rosanne and I experience, is the call to perseverance. We want to be among those who "hear the word in a spirit of openness, retain it, and bear fruit through perse-verance" (Lk 8:15). We know that God wants us to be faithful to his call even though we may never see the fruit of our labor. As we try to remember each day that this is Jesus' ministry, he will work in the hearts of those we minister to and in ways we may never see. Sometimes we have the privilege of seeing ways that his light shines to bring others closer to himself.

One such way was through an incident that happened in our Spanish youth group. We had just finished viewing with our young adults a video tape of the television special on Mother Teresa. A couple of young people in our group came in late and asked the youth leader to explain what the video was about. He replied, "If people would come on time, they would know what happens at our meeting!" Afterward both people walked out of the meeting and said they would never return.

After the meeting came to a close, I spoke to the lead-er, who was very upset over the incident. I tried to explain to him that things like this are bound to happen at times. I told him how it might be good if he could call them during the week to apologize. He seemed open to the idea.

The next day, after praying with Rosanne about this, I called one of the people who walked out of the meeting. She talked a lot about what had happened, and I could tell how angry and hurt she felt over the whole experience. At the end of the conversation, I felt as though I had to say something about forgiveness, although I didn't want to. I experienced a fear that she might reject me as she had rejected the youth leader, but I knew I had to say some-thing to her. I told her that I know at times it's hard to forgive, but maybe she could think about it. There wasn't much of a response after that, but I was relieved to know that she still wanted to stay in touch with us.

At the next youth group meeting, Rosanne and I noticed that the two young adults who had walked out at the previous meeting were not there. I asked the leader of the group if he had called them to apologize. He said that he hadn't been able to reach them, so we suggested to him that he write a letter to them asking for forgiveness.

We are grateful to God that the following week they both came to the youth group meeting. Reconciliation had taken place and it was certainly worth the effort!

In trying to start Lamplighter gatherings in our parish, forgiveness also seems to be something the children are experiencing. It's wonderful to hear the voice of a child say "I'm sorry" to another, and say "Do you forgive me?"

As LAMP ministers we don't see results such as these every day. The Lord Jesus continues to tell us not to be discouraged but just to be faithful in seeking his will in his ministry. Lord Jesus, thank you for the privilege of seeing the results of your light shining in others. Give us the grace to have confidence that you are working in the hearts of your people, even when we may not see it.

"A DUTY TO BE LOVING"
Bob Englert

I have been a LAMP minister for seven months, serving at Holy Spirit Parish in the South Bronx. Recently a film crew, making a documentary on the work of LAMP, came to our parish. During the interview, I was asked to describe my duties as a LAMP minister. The question was simple and certainly routine, but I hesitated to give what would have been my normal response to such a question. Somehow, to answer, "I work with the CCD, the youth

group, the lectors; I help at the shelter for the homeless,"
seemed inadequate.

The fact is that I do those things, but my hesitation
centered on the word "duty." Ministering to groups is certainly an important part of my work, but indeed my service
in the church is so very personal, and so very satisfying.
For me it is at the heart of what is means to be a Christian.

Therefore, I'd like to share what my "duties" are as a
LAMP minister:

- giving Rose, who is deaf and often insecure due to her
  handicap, a big hug at the time she really needed it;
- reading the scriptures to Mabel, an elderly woman who
  is dying of cancer;
- being with Louise during a court hearing, and helping
  her to think about Jesus at a time of crisis;
- staying up all night to keep an old boiler running so that
  the homeless men in our shelter will have heat;
- listening and talking with these men, as I did with the
  man who, when he first came, would sit by himself in a
  corner, looking extremely dejected;
- sitting in my room and praying that Francisco will be
  able to stop drinking;
- stopping by Mitch's house and asking if he would like to
  come to the retreat on Sunday, even though I feel he will
  not come;
- taking a walk with Fr. Ken when things get a little too
  hectic in the rectory;
- going to daily mass, asking Jesus to give me the help and
  strength to share his love with those who most need it.

When the interviewer asked me that question, these
were the people who were in my heart; these are the "duties" that God has entrusted to me. Living out the gospel,

as a LAMP minister, is like walking under a great light. Sometimes that light exposes things in me that I'd rather not see (and especially don't want others to see), but on the positive side that "light" is a beautiful and ennobling reality. It is, of course, the light of God's wonderful love, and so St. Paul's words to the Ephesians ring true for me: ". . . now you are light in the Lord. Well then, live as children of light. Light produces every kind of goodness and justice and truth" (Eph 5:8–9).

RECEIVING THE NEW LIFE OF JESUS

In the midst of severe hardships and uncertainty in their daily lives, a number of children living at the Martinique Hotel were baptized this spring. The Martinique is a shelter for about five hundred homeless families in midtown Manhattan where LAMP minister Sr. Emmanuel Palus, A.S.C., serves.

There was a family who attended mass each Sunday, but it was only after Sr. Emmanuel reached out to one of the older children in the family that she discovered none of the children had been baptized. When she asked the parents if they would like the children baptized, they joyfully responded. In their life of poverty, they had never lived in one place long enough to have any of their ten children baptized or instructed in the faith.

While the five oldest began to receive instructions, the five youngest were baptized one Saturday afternoon. We have often expressed the purpose of LAMP Ministries as complementing the physical and social supports of the poor through supporting their faith life. This was manifested so beautifully at this baptism when the parents chose one of the social workers in their welfare hotel to be the godfather of the children.

Through Sr. Emmanuel's presence and encouragement to this family and many others, children are being prepared for baptism, first communion, the sacrament of reconciliation, and confirmation at nearby St. John the Baptist Church.

We celebrate the new life God is giving these children through the sacraments and ask him to continue to fill their lives with his light and all good things.

HOMELESS FAMILIES HUNGRY FOR GOD
LAMP Minister Sr. Emmanuel Palus, A.S.C.

Already a year has passed since my first encounter with the poor and homeless of New York City and the beginnings of my service as LAMP minister at the Martinique Family Welfare Hotel in midtown Manhattan.

As a LAMP minister, I am very much aware of the call to share deeply in the redemptive mission of Jesus, to "bring good news to the poor," to "build up his kingdom." From the beginning I was drawn to LAMP because LAMP's mission, its goal, corresponds so much with my own community's charism, following the church's call to give "preferential option for the poor."

Each day I am exposed to the tragic consequences of poverty, rejection and homelessness. The spiritual, physical, emotional and mental scars, the utter frustration, discouragement, desperation, and a sense of uselessness, lack of self-esteem and self-worth, lack of motivation—these are all marks deeply etched into the faces and broken lives of so many of the homeless families. The children, especially, are victims of this tragic lifestyle.

The day is filled with crisis situations: people asking for food for their hungry children because their welfare check or food stamps didn't stretch enough; need for clothing and medical help; family problems and disputes; abused mothers and children; both single mothers and some single fathers struggling desperately to take care of the daily needs of their children.

I have found so many good, wholesome families who are eager to "get back in touch with God." My presence in the welfare hotel as a LAMP minister gives them this opening, this opportunity. I speak about Jesus with them as their source of hope and courage. Many are open to prayer. A lot of "faith-sharing" and prayer happens spontaneously in clusters in the area where I have a desk and a few chairs. Since I've been at the hotel, there have been many, many requests for Bibles. The word of God has been a source of much encouragement, and has provided many opportunities for sharing, discussion and prayer.

One of the greatest joys of my ministry has been the initiation of the religious education program for our hotel children and parents—set up in collaboration with nearby St. John's Church.

Babies and young children have been baptized; children of adequate age have been prepared for the sacraments of reconciliation and eucharist; others are being prepared for confirmation. Several of our young boys have been trained to serve as altar boys. Mothers and fathers have taken the opportunity to seek counsel and advice from the priests at St. John's. Without the presence of LAMP in this shelter, it is doubtful if any of this would be happening.

Being a LAMP minister has been a great joy to me as, through Jesus' presence, others have come to find some peace and hope in troubling circumstances. Desperate young mothers have found the courage to avoid abortions and find peace and joy in giving birth to the child God sent them—coming to a new appreciation of the value of the precious gift of life! Others have turned from drugs, determined to begin again for the sake of their children. A number of others, plagued by suicidal tendencies, driven to this state for various reasons, have sought counsel and help, and found strength to face life in the assurance of God's help and presence. Jesus continues to be savior!

A SEARCH FOR UNDERSTANDING
Senior Lamplighter Maria Scheuring

Sometimes the troubles and confusions of young people can best be understood by people their own age. That is what five juniors from Preston High School in the Bronx are trying to accomplish by getting to know a group of homeless teenagers from the Martinique Hotel. We are taking part in this senior Lamplighter outreach as part of our junior service program.

We organized a clothing drive in our school for the benefit of these teenagers and their friends, and we are preparing to meet with them to understand their thoughts and feelings about life while also explaining our own.

Our goal in this project is to discover what we have in common, and, as we do that, to make the message of the gospel more meaningful for all of us.

"YOUR PEOPLE WILL BE MY PEOPLE" (Ru 1:16)
LAMP Minister Gregory Fischer

On March 1, 1986, at Our Lady of Lourdes Church, on 142nd Street between Amsterdam and Convent Avenues, in an area that some consider Harlem, my first assignment as a LAMP minister began, but I made my first visit to the parish on a mild winter's morning a few weeks earlier.

The cold wind had stopped blowing and the winter sunlight had become warm to the touch. I was walking along Amsterdam Avenue with no particular destination in mind. Many people were on the street: white, black, brown, yellow. There were old people bundled up in winter clothing seated on sidewalk chairs and boxes, basking in the sun; idle men hanging out at storefront leisure clubs enjoying the weather, bantering, laughing, taking refreshment from bottles or cans which they held in brown paper bags. Little children, dressed not nearly warm enough, were running everywhere, laughing, shouting—black children, Spanish children. God's diversity is infinite. I became very aware that this ministry was going to be very challenging. Only through the prayers of others and the moment by moment guidance of the Holy Spirit was I going to be able to rise to that challenge.

Passing each group I sensed a subtle scrutiny. No one stared at me but I was sure I was being noticed. My imagination, you say? Maybe. But no! I definitely locked eyes with that man and then another and then another. I tried to exchange a smile or greeting, but before I could, they would look away. I thought, "Here I am, a foreigner in a strange place. I'm confident of God's call to serve the poor through LAMP, but is this the place?"

I remembered I felt like Gideon, in the book of Judges, putting down a fleece before the Lord. "O Lord, is this the place your message of good news has its greatest meaning? Give me a sign that you want me to work here."

It was lunchtime. I was tired and hungry and I needed a cup of good strong Spanish coffee. Here was a food shop—"Comidas" and "Cafe." I went in. There was one vacant stool near the front door. A shopping bag had been placed on it. I asked the customer on the next stool if I might sit there. Without a word or glance, he removed the bag and placed it on the floor between his feet. I thanked him and sat.

Again that very subtle scrutiny. O Lord, was I so self-conscious that I was attracting attention? Perhaps I appeared too curious, too observant. O Lord, help! A sign! It was as if Gideon were reminding the Lord of the fleece.

I was savoring the coffee, when suddenly the small man sitting next to me turned and, facing me directly, said in a picturesque speech I can't faithfully reproduce: "Isn't this coffee good?"

"Yes," I replied in surprise. "It's delicious. I love Spanish coffee."

Looking past him, I saw a row of heads now bobbing, seemingly in nods of agreement.

"They're listening," I thought.

"This be the best coffee around," my little friend continued as he poked me gently on the lapel.

"Thank you for telling me. I'm new to this neighborhood."

By now the bobbing heads were making listening noises. "Yes, yes!" "Uh-huh." "Good coffee."

"I come here every day!" my friend added.

And suddenly there was a group of friends talking about the menu, other restaurants in the neighborhood, the neighborhood at large and what nice weather we were having.

Now the waitress came to clear my place. I thanked her for the excellent coffee and asked for another, and when I turned to my companion I beheld one of the most beautiful expressions ever to appear on a human's face.

I must have gasped. I remember my thought, "Thank

you, Lord. Here is my sign. You've answered me." For the Lord had turned my Gideon's fleece into a welcome mat.

My fears subsided. I shouldn't have doubted it, but I saw that these are people just like me. I am their brother. I am here as a LAMP minister, needing the guidance of the Holy Spirit, to be their companion in getting more in touch with the presence of the Lord within each one, to help them become more aware of the love of God, as I become more aware of it through their love.

Spring 1988

CELEBRATING SEVEN YEARS
OF SERVICE

With March 25, 1988 being its seventh (a biblical symbol of fullness) anniversary, LAMP Ministries was honored to be invited to the March 20 Sunday eucharist at St. Patrick's Cathedral in New York City, celebrated by Cardinal John J. O'Connor. With the cathedral crowded with regular Sunday worshipers and visitors from around the world, Cardinal O'Connor recognized the contribution which LAMP is making to the church through its service with the poor.

As Cardinal O'Connor spoke of "Lay Apostolic Ministries with the Poor" (LAMP), he emphasized the word "with," noting his affirmation of this posture in our service of evangelization with the poor and homeless. At the liturgy LAMP ministers participated as lectors and processed with the offertory gifts to the cardinal.

After mass, Cardinal O'Connor invited the LAMP community to his residence for a reception. After speaking with Tom and Lyn, the cardinal greeted each LAMP minister and chatted informally with us while pictures were taken. It was a profoundly joyful experience.

Tom and Lyn mark as LAMP Ministries' birth the day they received a letter from Cardinal Cooke inviting them to come to New York from San Antonio, where they had been temporarily residing, to continue to research the dream they had of forming a service of evangelization with the materially poor. The letter arrived for the Marian Feast of the Annunciation, March 25, 1981.

SHARING FROM THE WELLSPRING OF OUR FAITH
LAMP Ministers Ben and Walda Javier

Ben had been a Fordham University philosophy professor for thirty-two years before serving in LAMP with his wife Walda.

The essential element in both of our lives since youth has been the living Catholic faith, through which we have found communion with God. This great gift pulsated within us a desire for sharing it.

Through LAMP Ministries we came to work at St. Gabriel's, a parish where there are many poor in New Rochelle, north of New York City. It is here that our desire for full participation in parish ministry is being realized.

Our pastor, Fr. John Dwyer, has involved us in ministry to the parents of the newly baptized. The infants exude the fragrance of heaven and the parents are so vulnerable to receive the message of the love of God for them.

We also teach a Bible study class and an inquiry/ refresher course on the Catholic faith which allows a systematic forum of study open to all.

The poor are those who are in need, and that includes all of us. Aware of our own poverty, we have come to serve and to share what has been given to us. One way we do this is through visiting the homes and apartments of people who live within the parish.

Our love is also given to Helen, she of the bright blue Irish eyes, who sits week after week in the nursing home counting her beads, praying for our work with others.

Our love is for Tiffany from Costa Rica, a beautiful nine year old who has kidney disease and is overjoyed to be preparing with us for her reception of the sacraments of baptism, penance and holy eucharist.

We share Karen's joy whose marriage will be validated in the church, allowing her to be reunited with our Lord in the blessed sacrament. And still "the harvest is ripe and the laborers are few" (Mt 9:37).

We were asked to teach the true devotion of Mary, according to St. Louis de Montfort, and have seen the fruits of this total consecration to Jesus through Mary. It gives apostles to the church. This helps us fulfill one of our roles as LAMP ministers, i.e. to be catalysts in training other evangelizers in the parish.

A recent tragic occurrence which has very much affected our ministry was the brutal beating and subsequent death of an eighteen year old boy, who was from a neighboring parish but for three days lay in the hospital across the street from St. Gabriel's. Hundreds of his classmates gathered at the grotto of Our Lady of Lourdes in the yard of St. Gabriel's. We led the rosary and shared their grief through those three days when he lay in a coma. This experience, deeply tragic as it was, drew the young people back to prayer. In their need they turned to God. They asked for help in praying, and one left a message to Mary in the grotto saying, "Please help us to pray for our friend."

In summary, we are most grateful for the opportunity afforded to us in this past year to share from the wellspring of our love and happiness—our Catholic faith.

LAMPLIGHTERS: LIVELY AND GROWING IN THEIR FAITH

This year we have had many opportunities to support teenagers in developing their Christian faith and sense of service.

Fifteen senior Lamplighters, high school students at five area secondary schools, participated in a weekend retreat this March. Most of these young people have been with Lamplighters for the past five years, learning through first-hand experience that those who suffer from poverty or homelessness deserve our respect and are capable of showing us how to live the gospel in the face of many hardships.

The theme of the retreat was simply "Jesus." Through a series of talks, discussions, prayer and meditation, a communal celebration of the sacrament of reconciliation, and a closing eucharistic liturgy, interspersed with sports, games, rest times, a party, good meals and tasty snacks all shared with the adult team members, these young people experienced a weekend of fun and faith-building. We believe that seeds of faith and caring were, by the grace of God, nurtured deeply within their hearts. As we follow up on this retreat experience, we see the senior Lamplighters eager to continue coming together to grow as Christians, be community for one another, and continue their service of care with those in need.

"MANNA" FOR THE DAY

A new and creative dimension of LAMP Ministries has recently been evolving. Raul Salgado, who has assisted his wife Jennie in her service as a LAMP minister, and who recently became a part-time LAMP minister himself, offered to donate and raise money to buy a canteen truck for LAMP. His dream was to use this truck to share food and Christian encouragement to those who live on the streets, especially in sections of the city where no soup kitchen is nearby.

When Raul went to purchase a truck advertised in the classified ads, he was told it was no longer available. As the LAMP staff prayed and searched with Raul for another truck, he noticed that the original truck was again listed in the classified ads. When he called the man, he was offered the truck for five hundred dollars less than the original price. Glory to God for his gracious assistance!

The Christian encouragement comes primarily from the volunteers who are helping, as they seek to be a loving, caring presence. They offer a copy of the gospel of John, or other leaflets containing passages from the scriptures, to anyone who would like to read. Songs of praise and hymns of mercy play gently in the background to further help the listeners to know of the compassionate love of Jesus. The food distributed is donated from various sources.

The truck is named "Manna," an old Testament name for the heavenly bread which the Lord provided the Israelites each morning in the poverty of the desert (Ex 16ff). Like its namesake, we offer some food for the day and the realization that God's mercy is renewed each morning, even in the midst of the deep suffering so many people endure in the "desert of poverty."

WITH HIS PEOPLE
LAMP Minister Norma Kane

Twice weekly, outside of St. Nicholas of Tolentine Church in the South Bronx, the Manna ministry takes place. Two or three of us from LAMP arrive around noon-time to meet those in the area who are in need, bringing with us a pantry truck filled with donated foods and a desire to share about the love of Jesus.

Manna started its evangelization ministry on May 13, the feast of Our Lady of Fatima, and continues to provide some small encouragement and refreshment to those who are without shelter or food or funds. The number to whom we minister varies. Toward the end of the month, when any money they have has run out, our supplies go quickly.

The food we offer has been made available through the generosity of many people or purchased through a food co-op. The food we give is given in the name of Jesus, and we know we are giving it to him. We see it in the eyes of those we serve. But more, we hear and believe his words: "I assure you, as often as you did it for one of my least brothers, you did it for me" (Mt 25:40).

The people we serve are not unfamiliar with God. When we remind them that "Jesus loves you" as we offer gospel booklets, they often respond quickly, "I know"—an immediate and certain response to an incomprehensible statement! We share more about God's love as they show an openness.

We know many now by name. We can ask the homeless where they sleep when it gets cold. (On rooftops, one told us.) We can congratulate a bewhiskered gentleman on his recent shave and haircut. We can encourage another to continue to stay away from alcohol when he tells us quite proudly that he has succeeded the last two weeks. We can offer to secure a clean pair of pants and good shoes for someone who needs to look presentable for an interview. We can encourage another to get to the detox center once she has decided she wants to.

They come to us (or are sent). We provide a little food—for the body and the spirit. And they leave—all too soon. I catch myself saying inwardly: Why are you leaving? Where are you going? Stay awhile. Can't we do something more for you?

These are God's people. He tells us he has come for the sick. Those who are well do not need him. And those who are sick find him, even if only for a moment when we are together. It is a privilege to serve him through serving his people. I truly wonder who is more blessed.

MANNA IN THE DESERT OF POVERTY

We park the Manna truck in an area where there are homeless who do not have access to a soup kitchen, and hand out simple food as well as share our faith with them as they are open to us, and give them a small scripture pamphlet or something about the Lord to take with them.

After they saw the numbers of neighborhood poor coming to the Manna truck, the parish, next to which we have been parking our Manna truck the past number of months, opened up its own soup kitchen for the poor in their area. This enabled us to move our ministry to another needy location. On our last day there one of the women who had regularly come for food came up to the LAMP minister and thanked her for the food but especially for her words about the love of Jesus. She said: "You may think we don't hear or listen to you when you tell us Jesus loves us or other things about him. We may not respond, but at night, when it's quiet, we remember and think about what you have told us about Jesus. Thank you!"

This ministry, as with all of life, is not without its humorous moments. Just today, I (Tom) was helping with the Manna ministry and a homeless man came by pushing his shopping cart of empty soda cans. The other LAMP minister said that he had come by other times. Even before I had a chance to say anything to him, he said quite definitively, as if anticipating what topic I might bring up: "I'm going to give my life to God . . . as soon as possible."

We feel that our primary purpose is to be a witness of the love of God. Hopefully the people will experience it through our interest in them, the food, or maybe just a smile. The Lord's love has been clearly extended through Manna volunteers like Bredhe Stallard, Eileen Fallon, Ann McElvaney and Phil Turgot. Norma Kane's orchestration of volunteers and her own commitment to the poor and hungry make Manna possible.

The Manna outreach operates two days a week and one Saturday a month. We have just been approached by another parish in the South Bronx, who would like us to bring the Manna truck to their parish at least one day a week to provide food for the homeless in their area. They are very aware that through this ministry more than physical food is given out. Our goal is to provide food for the whole person, their spirit as well as their body, for children as well as adults.

There is a newsletter that is put out through a South Bronx hospital, primarily by and for homeless and out-patient AIDS victims. Two of the men who work on it came by the Manna outreach one day, and as a consequence wrote a brief article in their newsletter. Some excerpts from the article: "Several weeks ago, I became acquainted with a group of people who are dedicated to helping the needy." They have "been out in the cold serving coffee and sandwiches to those willing to accept their generosity." "I was immediately impressed with the generosity of these [LAMP ministers], which prompted me to write this article." "If you should happen to be in this area . . . you will surely catch sight of their 'Truck of Plenty.' " "More than likely, you will be greeted by these kind, gentle, spiritually rich and generous people."

LAMP YOUTH EVANGELIZE
Maria Scheuring

It's Saturday, April 22, at 11 A.M., and a dozen or so senior Lamplighters gather at the LAMP Center, as they do the third Saturday of every month. The reason for their gathering is the Manna outreach. Through Manna we are serving people in front of St. Thomas Aquinas Parish in the South Bronx, where at last count over one hundred needy people line up on the street waiting for our arrival.

The food—sandwiches, loaves of bread, peanut but-

ter, jelly, pastries, along with hot soups and beverages—
are donated to LAMP by various stores and people who
just want to help the poor in some way. A very important
aspect for us youth is to actually talk with the people
about God and his love for them, and to give them pam-
phlets to feed their spiritual lives as well as their physical needs.

When we come back from this outreach, we ourselves
feel that we have gained much more than we have given.

THE SPIRIT SHOWS US WHAT TO DO
**LAMP Minister Eileen Connor,
who serves with the homeless**

I would like to give glory to the Lord for the way he
led me to act on behalf of a resident of one of the midtown
SRO (Single Room Occupancy) hotels where LAMP serves.

This resident, named Kyie, was a quiet woman whose
mental disability was apparent by the way she dressed and
her inability to speak coherently. Also, her hands and legs
looked as though they were being gnawed by something.
She did not cause any trouble with others, and was liked
by all who knew her.

However, from time to time I would knock on her
door to see how she was and bring her a cup of coffee.
This time when she opened her door, I became very upset
at seeing the roaches and mice which covered the floor
and the walls of her room. That night I couldn't sleep.
I kept praying that God would show me what to do. I
couldn't let her remain in that state.

In the past, when I had talked numerous times with

staff from different social agencies, they told me they couldn't do anything, because Kyie had done okay on a psychological evaluation. I couldn't let this situation continue. With the help of LAMP and the Archdiocesan Office for the Homeless and Hungry, another evaluation took place, and Kyie was taken to the hospital for treatment.

The change in Kyie over the weeks was wonderful to see. She looked like a different person, her face became more expressive and peaceful, and she began to be able to carry on conversations. Her skin began to heal.

I was so thankful that the Lord had been able to come to Kyie's aid. In addition, he provided a new place for her to live where there is support for residents.

This taught me more graphically that God doesn't want his children to live in degradation. He wants each person to know his or her dignity, to have new life, and he more than provides it when we seek him.

Another experience of Eileen's had to do with Randy and Suzette. They and their four children lived for three years at the Bryant Hotel, a welfare shelter in Manhattan for homeless families where Eileen serves. Gradually Suzette started associating with the wrong people and began using crack. She sold everything, even her wedding ring, to get the money for drugs. One of their children was born while Suzette was on crack. Three of their children were eventually taken from her and placed in foster homes, and their fourth lived with a relative. Randy kept trying to help his wife get off crack.

Eileen began visiting and praying with them, and also put them in contact with a local church in the Times Square area. It didn't happen immediately, but eventually, with Eileen's encouragement and support, Suzette stopped using crack and developed a relationship with Jesus in her life. Soon afterward they were able to find an apartment. Before they moved out of the shelter they were hosting a weekly Bible sharing group in their room. A few months after they moved into their apartment, the court allowed their children to return to them. They were so grateful to realize God's care for them.

A MINISTRY OF AVAILABILITY
LAMP Ministers Jim and Maure Rupp

In the spring of 1987 we experienced the call from God to serve him in a deeper way. We were living in Texas, had many wonderful friends, a home of our own, two cars, our jobs, and a comfortable lifestyle. After a discernment process, we were accepted by LAMP. We felt God calling us to a simpler lifestyle, so we resigned from our jobs, put our house up for sale, sold a car, and disposed of all our furniture.

Now our journey of faith continues here at St. Jerome's, a predominantly Spanish parish in the South Bronx. After a year here, we have some wonderful friends, brothers and sisters in Jesus, a feeling of being part of the neighborhood, and memories that will be with us always. Each day is different and challenging. Mornings, we may listen to a story of an elder's memories of the neighborhood, bring communion to the sick, or perhaps meet with our pastor, Fr. John Grange, to plan our evangelization activities for the week. Afternoons can find us sharing with a religion class in the school, leading the junior high youth group, or visiting someone in his or her apartment. Evenings can be our busiest time, as we meet with engaged couples, prepare families for baptism, and make home visits.

We also prepare lectors and eucharistic ministers for service, and teach a CCD class. We have met with small groups of parishioners in their apartments to share God's word, pray, sing, and enjoy a meal together. Along with LAMP minister Eileen Connor, we brought six teens to a youth retreat at Franciscan University in Steubenville, Ohio last summer.

There are always people who come to us with questions and problems, or who just would like to talk. We rejoice when someone thanks us for a prayer, or for listening to his or her story. We believe this is what our ministry is about: sharing and "being with" the poor—a ministry of availability. Through him, with him, and in him we are one in the Holy Spirit who guides and strengthens our ministry with the people of God.

Our pastor has been a guiding light as he makes requests and suggestions and shares his knowledge with us. We experience the grace he has for the parish and are blessed to have much freedom in spreading the good news of the love of Jesus. In humility, we see that much of our "success" as LAMP ministers is due to the loving work of the priests, sisters, and lay people who preceded us at St. Jerome's. We in turn are planting seeds which others who come later will harvest. It is enough that we remain faithful and obedient to the Lord.

We have learned to endure disappointment, frustration, and misunderstanding, as long as we hold fast to the divine presence and Spirit of Jesus. Daily prayer, both planned and spontaneous, connects us to our source. Each morning we pray the divine office with Fr. Grange, followed by the eucharist. We echo Paul who said, "I can do all things in Christ who strengthens me" (Phil 4:13).

MINISTERING AS THE LORD LEADS
LAMP Minister Sr. Rene Canitrot, O.P.

God is faithful! What God puts into our hearts we can find, if we seek. For me, this seeking has led me to LAMP— a loving community of men and women who wish to give over their lives to God in service to his poor ones. Through LAMP, I have come to Blessed Sacrament Parish in Newark, N.J. This is a parish where one is welcomed warmly, and it is possible to come to know the people because our numbers are small.

My days here are all different, and this is in part possible because Fr. Paul Schetelick, the pastor, encourages us to minister as the Lord leads. Some days are spent in the Blessed Sacrament food pantry where I, with volunteers, meet God's poor. We endeavor to give them more than they came for—namely, the word of hope and trust in God. As I am getting to know these brothers and sisters in Jesus, they are more and more open in inviting me to visit them in their homes.

Other days are spent at University Hospital where I am a volunteer in the pastoral care unit. There I meet the suffering in body and spirit and experience the power of Jesus' name. So often I meet persons who cannot communicate in English, and I rejoice that through the gift of being able to speak French and some Spanish I can pray with them in their own language.

One young man that I have met there is about thirty-five years old, and is dying from AIDS. At first I visited and prayed with him, and now we pray together. He tells me that before experiencing the presence of the Lord, he just "existed." Now, he is "living." Often when we pray, he doesn't say much, but just squeezes my hand. That says more than a thousand words.

One patient whom I was visiting asked me to visit a woman down the hall, who was just diagnosed as having brain cancer. When I went to see her, she was overwhelmed with grief at the thought of her children losing their mother. As we talked and shared, I was inspired to tell her that she has given her children so much love, but now she has a chance to give them the greatest gift of their lives—a witness of their mother continuing to have faith even in the face of deep suffering and death. This made a tremendous difference in her ability to deal with her circumstances with God's peace.

Now that I am in my second year in the parish I have come to know our parishioners and the neighborhood and realize more and more that the harvest is plentiful.

I am grateful to my religious community, the Dominican Sisters of Amityville, N.Y., for their generosity in giving me this opportunity to serve as a LAMP minister.

ONE OF OUR FAMILY

Several weeks ago, Marybeth went to visit the O. family in Brooklyn. They had moved to an apartment after having lived for three years in the Martinique Hotel, a shelter for homeless families. While at the hotel, they came to know Sr. Emmanuel Palus, a LAMP minister who serves at the Martinique. We asked the O. family (Mrs. Pat O. and Phillip, twelve years old, Johnny, ten, and Anthony, nine) to reflect on their experience of the ministry of Sr. Emmanuel:

> *Mrs. O:* Well, to begin, Sr. Emmanuel was always praying. I would see her often, and she thinks I didn't notice, because it was always to herself, but I did notice.

She tried to make everyone happy, and she did it from her heart.

I liked to buy her a cup of coffee, because I felt she really cares about my kids. I couldn't give her much, and she never asked, but I wanted to do that for her.

Phillip: She's a real nice lady. Sometimes she would share things with us, and she always remembered us on our birthday. When something was wrong she would take our hands, or she would take my mom's hand, and she'd say something that would cheer us up.

Johnny: She gave us pictures of saints and rosaries and would tell us stories. Sometimes she would help us with our homework. I liked to share things with her, and we would run to the store for her.

Anthony: She is helpful to us. She would always tell us that God was with us.

Mrs. O.: She is a close friend to us, one of our family. For a long time at the hotel I wanted my children to have religious instruction, but I didn't know what to do. It was when Sr. Emmanuel came as a LAMP minister to the hotel that she helped me get the children to St. John's for their religion class.

Anthony: Yes, when I made my first communion, she came to the mass and then we went to have something to eat.

Mrs. O.: It's hard not having a home to invite a special guest to, but we were happy that Sister came with us to eat to celebrate Anthony's first communion.

Anthony: You know what! For my first communion my mom went to the florist to buy me a flower to wear, but she didn't have enough money. She was sad that she couldn't get me one. When we were walking to the church we found a carnation right on the street. We couldn't believe it.

Phillip: One boy from the hotel went to Sr. Emmanuel and asked her where he could be an altar boy. She told me, and I took him to St. John's where I taught him what to do. He's the second boy that I've trained.

Johnny: The Capuchin, Brother Michael, who used to train the altar boys, gave me this crucifix. Look! I put it in the center of my room because the Lord comes first.

Mrs. O.: Sister is always helping someone, and she is nice to everyone. Sometimes I get angry and hurt because people aren't always nice back, but that doesn't stop her from helping them in whatever way she can. I think that's what a LAMP minister does.

We thank the O. family for giving us this interview. We ask the Lord Jesus to continue to pour out his love and mercy on the whole family and on all the families who are presently suffering through homelessness.

Spring 1989

JESUS SHINING FORTH
LAMP Minister Sr. Pat B. Scanlan, C.S.A.

> The Spirit of the Lord is upon me because he has cho-
> sen me to bring good news to the poor . . . (Lk 4:18).

Every time I reflect on these inspired words from
Luke, I am moved into the mystery of Jesus incarnate and
grateful for being called to share in the mission of Jesus
as a LAMP minister.

My service with the people of the parish of St. Joseph
in Yonkers, N.Y., enfleshes for me the vision of the good
news, Jesus Christ. Having experienced many deaths and
resurrections on my faith journey as a Sister of St. Agnes
for some thirty-five-plus years, and as a LAMP minister for
the last three years, I know that this good news is to be
both lived and loved. He is the only source of evangelization through whom the Spirit flows, allowing LAMP to
shine forth to enlighten my vision.

No longer do I just see the numbers of spiritually and
materially hungry and homeless who line up for the weekly food pantry or passively exist on the neighboring streets
of the parish. No longer do I just see the mugging of Agnes,
one of our Senior Club members, by a crack-filled addict
who is oblivious to the trauma perpetrated on another
human being, or just see the loneliness of the hospitalized
and aged's long-spent days and nights. No longer do I just

see the varying complexions of our parish family as I assist at liturgy, scripture prayer groups, prayers and material support for the bereaved, sick and homebound, or just see the subtle ethnic severances in our own Christian community that cause a cloud of injustice and unrest over our society.

No, this is Christ's suffering body, God's children, my brothers and sisters, with whom as a LAMP minister I am compassionately in labor to "bring forth good news" through concrete daily service of prayer and presence. Poverty is not a pretty picture of beauty, excitement and drama, and its companion, suffering, is the portrait of any person broken in body, spirit or dreams.

In my many experiences as a LAMP minister I have been privileged to walk with a terminal cancer-tormented patient, Natividad, who now intercedes for St. Joseph Parish to the Lord. I have walked with bottle-bored alcoholics, and with the recently evicted young couple with four children whose husband and father has lost his job and with it the will to live. I spend time with the Special Action Group of our parish that is striving to revitalize our neighborhood with social justice programs. My pastor, Fr. Patrick M. Carroll, who encourages others to use their gifts to build the kingdom, centers on the liturgy as the source of renewal, and so I am involved with lectors, eucharistic ministers and song leader ministry also.

Beauty and brokenness are key elements of every Christian parish community. Though seemingly contradictory, when they are blended together they portray a panorama of the face of Jesus in the daily people, events, and places of our lives. It is in the simple breaking of the bread of our life with others and sharing in the brokenness of each other's lives that we come to recognize Jesus shining forth in all his splendor and mercy. It is in this meeting that we know the healing wholeness of beauty personified.

I will be forever grateful to God for calling me as a LAMP minister to "bring the good news to the poor," for it is in this service that I have come to recognize Jesus in the beauty of his broken body!

HAVING AN "ANGEL" WITH US
Pat Sweeney

LAMP minister Pat Sweeney came to the United States from Ireland to serve with LAMP, and has returned to Dublin this spring. Pat served at two hotels for home-less families in Manhattan.

When I first met Trina in the lobby of the Hamilton Hotel one cold December day, I sensed that we would be good friends. She was twelve years old, and had an open, friendly manner with a winning personality. Her family, who lived in the welfare hotel for some time, had now moved to an apartment in Manhattan.

When she comes to visit her father who is employed by the hotel, she stops very often to talk with me about her school, which she loves, and the church choir where she sings on Sundays. She is very interested in learning more about the life of Jesus and his love for each one of us, no matter what creed, color or race we are. I introduced her to praying the rosary and explained to her that the rosary is a prayer based on scripture. Trina recited one decade of the rosary with me at lunch time one day, and even though she is a Baptist, she is very open to praying to the mother of God to ask her to intercede with Jesus for all her needs.

In the evening after school, some of the children in the hotel recite the rosary together, and I explain to them as simply as I can how Jesus, through the intercession of Mary, will help their families. Each Friday I also pray the rosary with an elderly couple in the hotel, and we pray for all the people in their difficulties and struggles which they are presently experiencing in their lives.

I was feeling a little discouraged one particular day, when Crystal, who is seven years old, came to talk with me in the lobby. I asked her if she loved Jesus, and she told me she did. She also told me that she prayed to the Holy Spirit to help her family, and that Jesus would protect her family from the devil who was very strong. What faith! The words of scripture, "Suffer the little children to come to me, for theirs is the kingdom of heaven" (Lk 19:14), came alive for me that day. Accompanied by Crystal, another LAMP minister and I spent the rest of the day visiting and praying with some families. The whole experience was like having a little angel with us for the day, and it had a wonderful effect on my service.

I marvel at the faith of the people and especially the children who exist in such difficult conditions. They are so open to the love of Jesus for them, and I feel privileged that the Lord has afforded me the opportunity of serving the poor through LAMP Ministries.

Through evangelizing in the hotels, I have experienced both success and disappointments, but the Lord has upheld me and delivered me through my own prayer life and through the support of the LAMP staff and all the LAMP ministers.

Through it all, my life has changed drastically. My presence seems to mean so much to these people who live in the hotels, something I have rarely felt before in my life. It is as if for the first time I am accepted for myself and not for my accomplishments. It has been a wonderful and healing experience, where I have experienced being evangelized by the poor.

I think of the words of Jesus, "The harvest is great but the laborers are few. Pray to the Lord of the harvest to send laborers into his harvest" (Mt 9:37). This is my favorite prayer, that others who have themselves experienced the deep and abiding love of Jesus in their lives will themselves share the good news that Jesus is alive and is risen with others who are hungry for God.

WE NEED MORE LAMP MINISTERS
IN THE CHURCH

Millie is a woman whose family lives across from St. Jerome's Parish in the South Bronx, where LAMP ministers Jim and Maure Rupp serve. We asked Millie to reflect on her experience of the Rupps' service as LAMP ministers:

Right from the time Jim and Maure were introduced by Fr. Grange at the Sunday masses, they showed a warmth toward all people of the parish as they greeted us. Feeling their openness, I stopped to greet them. Soon after, they invited me to visit them, and we began to talk more deeply.

One time when they came to visit me in my home, my son had had an accident, and I was very upset. They prayed with me, and whenever I saw them after that, they told me they were still praying. Thanks to their prayers, my son recuperated. Their support has meant so much to me.

I appreciate how they accept our suggestions and

put them into action. Once I had an idea that perhaps some people and families from the parish could get together regularly at one another's houses for dinner and sharing. Together we implemented this idea. People came and we began to be closer to each other. Eventually, this developed into a prayer meeting which we now have once a week. All their planning and organizing have brought people from the parish so much closer together. Through them our relationship with God has grown. We need more LAMP ministers like them in the church.

Iris and her daughter April (age six) also live in St. Jerome's Parish. Here are their reflections on Jim and Maure's service:

Iris: I had just started going back to church when Jim and Maure began to serve in St. Jerome's. Because I was taking instructions to receive my first communion and confirmation, I got to see them in the rectory every week. It was so good just to be around them. They are always so friendly. They are always there for us and they never put us off. When they go away, like for a vacation, people miss them very much. I see that many people in the parish and the neighborhood are touched by them. Also, through their work I've met other people and have become friends with them. They help me feel that I belong here in the parish.

I feel much closer to God because of them, not confused anymore. I have a friend who is a Jehovah's Witness, and that left me with a lot of questions. Jim helped me to understand our faith better, and he even gave me a book that explains the difference between my beliefs and my friend's. I am very glad they have started a prayer meeting. Sometimes I am very busy and I don't think that I have the time to go. But then when I do go, I experience God's presence there, and I come back happy.

April: I like Jim and Maure. They are nice people. I like Maure because she always makes us feel happy when we see her. She gives us such a big hello, and is so joyful.

Iris: Maure also wrote April and me letters, which helped us love and appreciate each other more. I thank God that they have come into our lives, and that they are LAMP ministers.

"YOU ARE PRECIOUS IN MY EYES" (Is 43:4)
LAMP Minister Eileen Connor

The week before Easter, a little girl named Precious, who lived in the hotel for homeless families where I serve, wanted a coloring book that was in the Health Office. I told her that we needed that one, and that she might ask God to put one in her Easter basket. (The Social Service workers and others of us serving in the hotel had asked a Woolworth's store to make up four hundred Easter baskets for the children at the hotel.) When I said that to her, Precious, standing at the window and looking up, responded by saying, "God can't hear me. He's too far away." "Sure, he can," I encouraged her. Then she said, "Well, even if he can, I don't trust him." I told her that he was the one we could trust the most. I prayed with Precious, asking God for a coloring book for her, and she repeated the prayer after me.

In my own mind, I was planning how, when the Easter baskets came, I was going to put one aside for Precious and put a coloring book in it. However, when the Easter baskets came from the store, all of them had a coloring book in them! I was so grateful to see God's faithfulness to Precious, and to each child I am here to serve.

A FURTHER STEP
Fr. Frank Pavone

God constantly renews his holy church, calling her to her fundamental mission of evangelization, and making the words of the great commission echo in the heart of all the members: "Preach the gospel to every creature!" This call is crystal-clear in the documents of Vatican II, and in Pope Paul VI's exhortation *Evangelization in the Modern World.* In the years before I entered the seminary, as I read these documents and brought their message to prayer, I was seized with restlessness, with a deep yearning to evangelize. My heart was burning within me, and I begged the Lord for greater opportunities to announce his gospel. In the echo of such prayers, I discovered LAMP Ministries, which gave me those opportunities. Announcing the gospel door to door, and helping people struggle along from unbelief to saving faith, was a marvelous preparation for my priesthood—in terms of both my present evangelizing and my work of forming the laity to spread the gospel.

After completing a year of service with LAMP I was accepted into the seminary, and this spring was ordained a priest for the archdiocese of New York.

A NEW START
LAMP Minister Ed Greene

I began serving full-time with LAMP Ministries seven months ago. I visit homeless families at the Hamilton Hotel in Harlem, and also one day a week I visit those who reside at Goldwater Hospital, a nine hundred bed state hospital for the severely disabled.

I could not be happier with what I am doing, and I wonder why I have not taken the step to do this sooner. I have met many wonderful people. By seeking Christ every day through this ministry I have been discovering more of who I am. It is a joy to share with others the most important gift—Jesus, through faith, hope and love which he gives us.

The one hundred and fifty homeless families that live at the Hamilton Hotel must cope with so many difficult circumstances at once. At times it is easy for others to come to judgment about their goodness and their concern for their children, but I have seen first-hand how much they love their children and worry about them. Over the summer many of the children were away attending a camp which city agencies arrange. It was a little lonely for me without the children, but for the parents it was much more sad. When the buses bringing the children home were barely within sight of the hotel, one of the mothers caught sight of it and alerted the others. It was very moving to see the mothers literally jumping up and down on the sidewalk in front of the hotel because their children were back!

One nine year old boy named Bruce, who lives at the hotel, had become friends with me over the weeks. One Sunday he saw me bringing some of the children from the hotel to mass at the nearby Catholic church. He asked if he could come. When I sent him to ask his mom, she said yes, and Bruce came back, bringing his little cousin Germaine. They have come several times with me. One Sunday Bruce turned the tables on me. I had other obligations, and was not planning to take the children to mass that day. Bruce brought his cousin to the rectory where I am living. He rang the doorbell, and when the pastor answered he asked for "Mr. Eddie." When I came to the door, he asked if I was ready to go to mass with them! I know Jesus must be very touched by Bruce's sincere interest in God and worshiping at mass.

Just recently at Goldwater Hospital, I was visiting a man named Jim, with whom I had never talked before. His ability to speak is very impaired, and as I was struggling to understand what he was trying to say to me, what I think was a movement of grace enabled me to grasp that he was shouting "Holy communion!" over and over again. It was a tremendous joy for me to bring the body of Jesus to this man who was crying out for him with his whole heart.

Some weeks back a couple at the hotel for the homeless shared with me that they were planning to get an abortion. The wife had been sick, and they were fearful that the baby may not be normal. Through much encouraging discussion and prayer and after putting them in contact with an appropriate office in the archdiocese, they changed their mind and decided to have the baby. The wife then found out that her sickness was simply the flu. Thank you, Lord! I continued to visit with the couple, and about two weeks ago the husband shared with me that he was so happy to have one friend. He had spent some time in prison and really felt he never had a friend. This past weekend this same man came to me and said he wanted to become a Catholic. What joy there is when just one person commits his or her life to God and wants to become part of the faith community.

A GREAT NEED FOR GOD
LAMP Minister Sr. Judith Mahoney, R.S.H.M.

It's been a year now since I have been serving at Immaculate Conception Parish in the South Bronx. In that time I have seen tremendous need all around me, and I have experienced great joy at the eagerness of the people to pray and turn to the Lord for help. Each day is different. I don't have a set schedule, but have learned that flexibility is very important, as I never know who will be walking through the rectory door.

I have met many homeless people, many unemployed, people trying desperately to get off drugs and searching for programs which might help them, people searching for apartments, for clothing, for medical help. Even more, I meet many who are searching for a human being with whom to talk. There is a great need for spiritual food, for God, and for the church in these people's lives.

I learned, too, that there are so many senior citizens "imprisoned" in their apartments because of their fear of and experiences with violence in the neighborhood. I try to set time aside to visit and pray with them. I bring them holy communion and provide any help that I can.

Margaret, a woman whom I visit, was ninety-three years old and had no one else in the world. She begged me to help her. Through much prayer I was able to find a nursing home where she might live in more peace for her remaining days.

Housing seems to be the most widespread problem. So many people live in rat-infested apartments, and in buildings which are unsafe, hazardous to health, and heavily plagued with drugs. One woman recently came to talk with me, desperate to find another place to live. She was living in a rat-infested room with her epileptic daughter. I prayed with her, asking God to open some door for her, and I asked the LAMP community to pray also. I have just heard that a nearby apartment building, newly renovated, will soon be available. We are hopeful that this family may be able to move to this new building.

When I suggest to different people that we pray together for their need, it is a privilege to see the joy which fills their faces at being offered this opportunity. More than one person has said to me that no one has ever said this to them before.

I have visited families who had been homeless and finally were able to find housing in our parish. When I visit them, they usually do not have furniture, yet they are always welcoming and warm. I help them in whatever way I can, sometimes helping them find jobs, and preparing them to have their children baptized.

Something about which I am very enthused is the RCIA. I am working with one of the priests of the parish, and we presently have twelve candidates. I very much look forward to the journey with them over the months as they prepare to receive the sacraments of initiation at the Easter vigil.

Some of the most striking experiences that LAMP ministers have often involve their contact with children, and the openness of these children to a relationship with God—from a child running to greet a LAMP minister, serving in a welfare hotel, with the exclamation: "I want to be like you," to the excitement of a homeless child when he discovers that he can be an altar boy, to a child in a South Bronx parish who said: "I like to see the LAMP minister. I always feel happy after that."

These are very simple experiences, but experiences that pierce through the sophistication we sometimes have about our faith. No doubt that is a part of the reason Jesus was so strong about children not being excluded from having a relationship with him—they can teach us so much about a simple, uncomplicated, trusting love for God. When we discover the beauty of a child's faith, we realize that we shouldn't spare any effort in helping them come to know the love of Jesus in their lives.

Sr. Judith also recounts how she spent many weeks working with a young child with an emotional problem which did not allow the child to eat solid food. The mother wanted so much for her son to receive his first communion, but it just seemed impossible, given this condition. The night before Sr. Judith first visited her apartment, this mother was crying out to God to somehow let her son receive the eucharist. This LAMP minister met over and over with the child, visiting, instructing, praying, encouraging, and helping him practice to swallow tiny pieces of an unconsecrated host, until he was finally able to swallow enough to consume the wafer-like host. One can imagine the great joy for this child and his family when he was able, for the first time, to walk to the altar and receive his first communion. The LAMP minister truly did prepare this child to "receive the body of Christ."

At another time Sr. Judith was aware of a seventeen year old girl who, from time to time, would come around the rectory. It was known that she carries a large knife in her purse, is a heavy drinker of alcohol and has been kicked out of most of the schools in the South Bronx.

One day the LAMP minister saw this girl at mass, sitting a few pews ahead of her. Sr. Judith asked the Lord to show her what to do and how to help this girl, whom she knew was not a Catholic. After mass she went to her office in the rectory. A few moments later, the girl came in behind her. In a rough voice the girl said she wanted to talk to her. In the beginning of the conversation the girl's hostility came out, saying she wouldn't be happy until she made blood flow through the use of her knife. Through the LAMP minister's sensitive listening, loving and firm responses, and witness about Jesus, the girl eventually softened and expressed her interest in becoming a Catholic. Sr. Judith made it clear that she would have to stop carrying the knife around and stop drinking. The girl left, saying that she wouldn't come back. A few days later she did, however, indicating her desire for strong direction and a relationship with God in her life.

Sr. Judith has been meeting frequently with this girl. Slowly, with God's help, her life is changing. She is getting back into school, and is finding peace in her heart through a relationship with Jesus.

HIS FACE HAD BECOME RADIANT
LAMP Ministers Jim and Maureen McGurty

As LAMP ministers, we are serving at St. Joseph's Social Service Center in Elizabeth, N.J., which seeks to meet the material needs of the poor and homeless.

Our evangelistic involvement in all of this has been an ongoing presence at the Center, which includes visiting with people who come in so as to be a faith support to them, starting a weekly prayer meeting, visiting people who are hospitalized, assisting in the distribution of food, and offering hospitality to those coming to the soup kitchen.

We have been able to institute a program of home visitation for those who are no longer able to come to the Center for services. We also give support and follow-up through prayer and dialogue with some who have taken the necessary steps to overcome their addiction to drugs and alcohol.

Each person has a story. For instance, Dan is a young Vietnam veteran who was an alcoholic when we met him. He had come into the Center in bad shape and was talking rather wildly about putting a thousand dollars on a horse. We began to talk with him and at one point asked if he might like to have us pray with him. He said "yes." We did pray over him, and that was it. We didn't see him again for two weeks.

Two weeks later he came into the Center, calm and coherent. He said to us, "Well, it worked. I've been sober ever since you prayed with me." He got a part-time job in a local church, and we occasionally saw him on the street.

We met the minister of the church where Dan was working just the other night. He told us that Dan had been placed in a vocational training program. "He looks wonderful these days," the minister confided. "He has been sober now for six months." We realized that it was six months ago that we prayed with him, and we glorify the Lord for his healing love.

Just recently we had an incredible experience with a man (we'll call him John) who is homeless and lives in a cardboard box on the street. He is forty-six years old, consumes much alcohol, and told us he had degrees in anthropology and psychology. He came to the Center because he said he had ruined his life and wanted to be committed to a mental institution. As he came several times, the only person he wanted to talk with was Jim, because, he explained: "You are the first person who has treated me like a man."

One night John came into the Center, babbling incoherently. Jim listened to him, and had a sense that he should ask Maureen to join them. John agreed to this, and they talked some more. Jim suggested that they pray. John wanted to ask God to change his life, and Jim told him that as long as he was sincere, God would honor his request. So John himself prayed aloud, asked God's forgiveness, and then began to shake. We became a little alarmed that perhaps he was going into DTs from the alcohol, and maybe needed medical attention. We decided to get a staff person who was more familiar with the signs of this. When Edie came, John looked up at us, and his face was radiant, like Stephen's as described in the scriptures. His eyes were clear; he was sober, calm and coherent. He said, "I don't need a doctor. I have Jesus. I'm not sure what happened, but something sure did." We were very touched and graced by that moment, maybe even more than he. We haven't seen him again, but we remember him in our prayers, and ask if you would remember him also.

We have discovered, like many LAMP ministers before us, that as we attempt to evangelize the poor, in fact we are the ones who are evangelized and the spiritual and emotional support we receive from LAMP and other LAMP ministers enhances and deepens our ministry. Without the support our ministry would not be as fruitful and fulfilling.

A CHANCE TO GIVE
LAMP Youth Malissa Scheuring

The Manna outreach has given us, the youth, a chance to give of ourselves to others who have so little. They are so poor, yet so rich in terms of what they give us. We learn from them and always seem to leave with more love than we came with.

A few young people who have shared in this ministry had these things to say:

"Helping the poor, and realizing they too possess lives of substance, can only enrich us."
—*Robert Kahwaty*

"I'm glad to get a chance to work with Manna. It is a way for me to help out the less fortunate."
—*Maria Asedillo*

"I enjoy working with Manna. You get to see Jesus' message of 'Love one another' in action."
—*Kristen Murphy*

Spring 1990

WE HAVE HEARD HIS NAME
Sr. Elvira Leal

LAMP Minister Sr. Elvira Leal, a Religious of the Sacred Heart of Mary, has served with LAMP since 1987 at the Prince George Hotel, a residence for homeless families.

Since I began my service with LAMP two and a half years ago, I have met many people, most of them homeless, who have impressed me deeply. Perhaps the most vivid memory I recall is with a young homeless couple at the hotel, ages seventeen and eighteen, who were expecting their second child. I got into a conversation with them about baptism, which led me to ask them, "Do you know who Christ is?" "No," they responded. "We have heard his name, but don't know who he is." The girl told me, "My grandmother told me God exists, but that's all I know."

I began by telling them that Jesus came on earth for each one of us, to suffer and die so that we could be united with God, and be happy forever. He loves us so much that he would have come even if there were only one person on earth. As Christians, we live our lives for God, so we can be with him forever.

Gradually I began to share about Jesus with them. At one point the young woman, with joy in her eyes, exclaimed to me: "No one ever told me what Jesus did for me!" A miracle was happening in her heart. The scripture verse almost spontaneously comes to mind: "And how can they hear unless there is someone to preach to them?" (Rom 10:15). This couple is now taking instructions to be baptized and they are having their child baptized.

An immigrant family that I came to know was extremely poor, and had no one in this country that they could even talk to, or from whom to receive support. I saw how much help they needed, and I tried to be of assistance by going to thrift stores to get some simple, basic things for them, like a hot plate, dishes, and clothes.

When they were leaving the hotel for homeless families, they stopped by to say that they wanted to become part of the Catholic Church. People from other churches knocked on their doors to ask them to come to their services, but I was the only one who wanted to spend time with them, visited them in their room, and acquired for them some material aid. I thank God for the grace that he gave them.

One day I got into a conversation with an eight year old homeless boy, and when I mentioned God to him, he told me not to "talk about God. My mother doesn't like God," he said, "because he killed my little baby sister."

I proceeded to tell him that his mother was mistaken. "God loves us so much, he would never kill anyone. But he does know what is best for us, and he must have had a plan for your little sister, to be like a 'little angel in heaven' to pray for you, and so he allowed her to die."

The more I talked, the more the little boy seemed to understand. When he was leaving, I reminded him to tell his mother that God loves them and didn't kill her baby. I hope he did.

There was a lady at the hotel who had tremendous pain in her knee and she could barely stand. I asked her if she would want me to pray with her, and she said "yes." I told her that she had faith and God would heal her. I asked her to picture Jesus touching her knee as I prayed.

Later that afternoon, a little boy came running down the hall, and when he saw me, he asked, "Are you the sister who prayed with my mother this morning?" I told him I was. "My mother is fine now. She is walking around."

The next day his mother came by to tell me that she was better because of my prayers. I told her that it was her faith that allowed the Lord to heal her, and that made her very happy.

Since I have been with LAMP, I have noticed that I have become more trusting in God. I used to become anxious if the bus was late, or if circumstances changed suddenly, or if something wasn't working out. Now I realize that it is all in God's hands and he will allow everything to work for good, so I don't have to worry. This gives me much peace.

"May this sharing of evangelization be for God's glory, and the good of all."

"THAT I MAY BE IN HIM" (Phil 3:9)
Teresa Hougnon

LAMP Minister Teresa Hougnon, who graduated from West Point, was assigned to Germany, and worked with "Teens and Twenties Encounter Christ" before coming to LAMP.

Just a short time after I left Buena Vista, Colorado to come to LAMP Ministries in New York, my home town newspaper ran a five-column feature article entitled "Hougnon Follows Her Faith to New York." Now, looking back on the ten months that have passed since, I believe a more accurate headline would have been "Hougnon Goes in Search of Her Faith." I had contacted Tom and Lyn and Marybeth initially in September of 1988. Their response was open, and after visits and discernment they invited me to come and respond to what I perceived as God's call for me. And so I did come to New York, somewhat dragging my feet nine months later, knowing well in my head, but not in my heart, that my faith would blossom in service to others.

St. John Cantius is a small parish in East New York in the Brooklyn diocese. The active parish is ninety percent Hispanic and ten percent Haitian-American. I realized very early in September that these people would teach me much more than how to speak Spanish. As I settled into the parish, I saw their day to day existence in a violent neighborhood as living faith, and I began to recognize my adjustment to that same neighborhood as bold ignorance. I had much to learn from the people in the parish.

My first adventure was to contact by telephone those adults who had expressed interest in becoming full members of the Catholic faith. After a few mild affirmative answers, one abrupt "no," and a few disconnected numbers, I encountered Ella K. With abundant enthusiasm she responded, "Yes, I do want to be baptized." Ella continued sharing with me over the telephone about her recent illness and hospitalization which led to a promise she had made to God to be baptized. She fully intended to keep that promise and wanted her son also to be baptized. I

welcomed her in advance and repeated to her the time
and date of the first RCIA class. As if the enthusiasm had
deflated, she replied quietly, "If it is the Lord's will, I'll
be there."

Ella did make it to the first class and could not thank
me enough for having called and invited her. I remember
thinking to myself, "If this is evangelization, it's not so difficult." As the months passed, Ella attended class each
week if it was "the Lord's will," and many times it wasn't.
Meanwhile, I was finding out, in other areas, that evangelization was difficult for me.

We operate a food pantry for emergency assistance at
the rectory. This activity provides the face to face contact
with people that is essential to evangelization. Henceforth
I became the "keeper of the key" and the most requested
person in the rectory, for as soon as I "assisted" one individual, five more would arrive at the door. A struggle arose
within me because I knew that only through faith in Christ
could I give each individual food without obligation of any
sort. Otherwise, to require their identification, their re-
ferral, or their "story" meant not only asking questions
but answering theirs. And to answer their questions meant
giving them information or directions as well as giving
them hope in a society that is willing to help them. So I
struggled with faith in Christ and also my hope in society,
needing both to face their people. I found that neither my
faith nor my hope was very strong.

As RCIA classes continued, Ella grew more enthusias-
tic about her approaching baptism. Talking with Ella, I
sensed that her enthusiasm was rich with anticipation and
unhampered by a lack of deep understanding. Never did
she cease thanking me for that telephone call and telling
me how nice I have been to her. When the time came for
the liturgies involving the catechumens, she would say to

me, "Now you're going to be there so I know what to do," and "You have to remind me so I don't forget what time I'm supposed to be there." While Ella was depending on me to be with her through this journey, I was witnessing in her a lesson that I had long ago forgotten or maybe never really understood. True faith begins with simplicity:

> . . . that I may be in him, not having any justice of my own based on observance of the law. The justice I possess is that which comes through faith in Christ. It has its origin in God and is based on faith (Phil 3:9).

For twenty-eight years I have been Catholic. When I was fourteen I received the gift of faith. Because my head is stronger than my heart, I have lived more through observance of the law, complicating a life that should be lived in faith. Now, having committed myself to spreading the message of Christ, I find my own faith to be very weak. But Ella has shown me the place to begin to rebuild my faith, to begin with simplicity. And if it is the Lord's will, as Ella believes, my faith will always remain simple, but grow in strength every day. What I have come to realize is that, uncomplicatedly, it requires obedience to answer God's call to evangelize the poor, it requires honesty to answer God's call to evangelize with the poor, but it has required humility to answer God's call to be evangelized by the poor, humility "that I may be in him."

WITNESSING TO YOUTH

Probably every adult generation has been concerned about their youth, about the influences on their lives, about their choice of the long-term good, not just the immediate gratification, about their choosing the truth of the gospel in their lives. Our generation certainly is no different, and we would probably say that due to drugs and moral degeneration we have more reason to be concerned about today's youth than ever before.

If one is a parent, you have probably been told many times by well-meaning friends and relatives that your children "will turn out fine." People want to give encouragement and hope, but we know that children don't turn out fine, at least what we mean by fine, unless they make a commitment to Jesus in their lives and they seek to live a gospel life.

God can touch their lives without any help from any of us, but that doesn't seem to be his method. He usually works through another person. All parents hope and pray that their children will be influenced by someone they might meet who will attract them into living a moral, faith-filled life. We know that that's the only way that they will be truly happy in their lives.

LAMP minister Ed Greene serves as a faith presence in a welfare hotel for homeless families in Harlem. One of the things Ed does with the children who periodically gather around him by his little desk in the small lobby of this rundown hotel is have them color pictures of the life of Jesus. He started taping the pictures up on the wall around his desk, and eventually they decorated the entire lobby. No one disturbed these pictures, wrote on them or ripped them down. The hotel manager didn't even complain, and the residents seemed to respect these pictures of Jesus so prominently displayed. The children are providing a faith environment to greet homeless families as they walk in and out of the hotel.

As members of the body of Christ, we are church together. We are responsible for each other. Our children may be grown and gone from our home, or they may be at home and we may feel very inadequate in affecting their lives with faith. But, while never giving up on our own, possibly there are other youths, neighborhood youth, young people we see at the supermarket or on the street, to whom we could make a conscious effort of being witnesses to the gospel. If all Christians felt a responsibility for youth and took active steps to witness to them about our faith, that would set free a tremendous faith-power in our society. We pray that this book will motivate and encourage you to some faith witness to the youth that touch your life.

Fall 1990

"TELL US HOW GOD CHANGED YOUR LIFE!"
Julio DeMasi

LAMP Minister Julio DeMasi, from Morgantown, West Virginia, served in a medical clinic for the poor in El Paso, Texas before coming to LAMP.

A year and a half ago I was looking for a way to be with the poor on a very personal basis. I wanted to be a presence, to be able to witness to my faith, as well as serve practically. When I heard about LAMP, I became convinced that this was the ministry that I was looking for, even though, to be honest, New York was the last place on earth where I wanted to serve. However, after I took time to discern what God was saying to me, that he was indeed calling me to evangelization with the poor through LAMP, I packed my bag and headed for New York.

St. Rose of Lima, a materially poor parish in upper Manhattan, an area notorious for drugs, is where I have been serving. When I first began, the pastor asked if I would work with the youth of the parish. While I knew that it would be a very challenging ministry, I believed that was God's direction for me. In addition, I also serve with LAMP's Manna outreach twice a week, a ministry that provides food and spiritual nourishment to the homeless in the South Bronx through the use of a canteen truck.

This past year has been a difficult one for me for several reasons. In the past, I was always comfortable relying on the leadership of others, and I did not have to take much initiative. I have also never worked with youth before. I had felt that there is so much risk involved in that ministry. They don't hide their reactions, and it has been a struggle for me to get over the fear of rejection. Over the year, as I have kept reaching out, I don't see so much change in the youth, but I see that God is changing me. When I take the initiative, it's a victory for me, even if I don't see many results.

Right after making a second year commitment, something happened. The Sunday I was getting ready for the first youth meeting of the school year, I was just not prepared to face these young people again. I prayed to the Lord and said, "Lord, I just don't have what it takes to be a youth minister, to lead these young people to you. You have to do something. You have to lead them." Something happened then. I felt that I had released the situation into the Lord's hands, instead of taking the full burden myself.

That night we had a real free-wheeling meeting, kind of wild, yet I experienced the Lord very much in it. At one point I said that someday I'll tell them about my conversion experience. They insisted that I tell them right then. "Tell us everything—what you were like before, what happened to you, what your life is like now!" And so I was able to witness to the love of Jesus in my life. I also was able to share with them in a clear way the church's teaching on sexual morality.

Since that meeting, I'm beginning to sense that a corner is being turned. Because of all the ways I had tried and failed, but kept trying over the year, it gave me ground to build on. Now they seem ready to take things more seriously. I certainly see the necessity of trusting more in God, being faithful to prayer and to more openly sharing the gospel whether I think they will accept it or not. I am encouraged that the Spirit is leading the way for these young people who need him so much.

"I KIND OF LIKE GOD"
Zoila Carvajal

LAMP Minister Zoila Carvajal, a young woman from Manhattan, is serving in Our Lady of Victory Parish in the South Bronx. "Yahweh knew me before I was born, in my mother's womb He pronounced my name" (Is 44:1).

When does the Lord call us to follow him?

Take Enrique: ten years old, tall, broad-shouldered, sensitive, bright. He is seeking full initiation in the church. "I don't like to fight," he says almost apologetically, but then emphatically, ". . . and I am not going to! I remember I saw Jesus in a movie once and they beat him up. . . . I just don't like to hurt people."

Ten year old Lavenia came to us seeking answers about her deceased father. "Where is he?" she wanted to know. With long pigtails and big, brown expressive eyes, Lavenia explains: "At school they call me a 'nerd' because I like to come to church." She then whispers, "I kind of *like* God." She is also picked on at school because she's "easy to hit." "But I just let 'em," she says. "I'm just *tired* of fightin'."

Brenda, eleven, and her sister Idalia, thirteen, arrived at our doorstep with a non-stop chain of questions about the church. And why not? "We love Jesus," says Idalia, "and if we're going to be baptized it has to be in the 'right' church." "We have to be picky," says Brenda. "After all, this is a lifelong decision."

Now Florita, a seven year old catechumen, doesn't really have any questions but she does call God "Daddy" as easily and freely as Jesus himself did. In her fragile, sweet baby voice she explains: "My real Daddy doesn't visit me, so God *has* to be my Father now." "Why are you in church?" I ask her. Florita gives me a blank look. "Because God is here and I want to be with him—to visit my family."

The other day I tried praying with this group of young people for the very first time. "Will he talk back?" asked seven year old Patricia. "You *promised* us he'd talk back!" I tried to explain to little Patty that praying was not like a séance, that God probably would not rattle the windows or talk back aloud, but that we could still hear him if we listened in our hearts.

Carmen giggles throughout the prayer. She is talkative, street-smart and precocious. When I look at her she says almost angrily: "Why don't God help the poor people? My mother helps poor people . . . why don't God?" "Do you help them, Carmen?" I ask. "Yes. I feel sorry for them . . . it's not fair. Sometimes I give them money and my friends say I'm stupid." "Are you?" "No," she says defensively, but then adds quietly, "I don't know *why* I like to help them. Do you think I'm stupid?"

These children have never known the Lord, not formally, but it was clear to me that the Lord had already claimed them for himself. He placed them at the doorstep of Our Lady of Victory Church—to be washed, anointed and fed with his sacraments, to give them an alternate world to their world of fear, pain and violence. They are here so that we may love them. They are here to evangelize the church. Some people are baffled and disheartened at seeing the evil around them and ask themselves: "Why?"

But I ask: In a city where evil and despair are common, how does one explain the *goodness,* the innate good in these children, for example. What are the "I don't know why's" and the "I can't explain's" of their good actions?

St. Vincent de Paul once said that "the poor take the place of the Son of God on earth because he chose to be poor." If this is so, then these South Bronx children, some of whom are one step up from homelessness, take the place of the Christ child. What Christian heart does not melt at the thought of the baby Jesus being born in a manger covered with dirt and flies? How many of us would not have longed to bathe his little feet, or help him get dressed, or read him Bible stories? (One wonders about all the "treasures" stored in Mary's heart.) Yet I wonder how many times was the child Jesus beaten at school because he was "different" or he "didn't like to fight"? Was he teased because he "kind of liked God," his "Daddy," or because he was "poor and from a strange family"? I see in every child a Christ child waiting for a mission from God. The Lord calls them even from the womb.

For twenty-seven years I have been pondering life's most complex questions. I have gone from cradle Catholic to radical atheist and back to the cradle. One of my greatest joys as a LAMP minister has been to form the children's catechumenate group of the RCIA. What can be more Christian, I think, than to serve children, those little people who live in a forced state of humility, whose happiness depends on others, who are often victimized and abused simply because they are small and weak. It was when I embraced being a child of God that I was liberated and found the answers to all the questions I had asked. I found that the key to a successful Christian life is humility and obedience to God, to surrender to his word—only with the help of his Spirit.

A PILGRIMAGE OF FAITH
Bob Lucas

*LAMP Minister Bob Lucas, serves at St. Charles Bor-
romeo Church in Harlem.*

It was by faith that Abraham obeyed the call to set out
for a country that was the inheritance given to him
and his descendants, and that he set out without
knowing where he was going. By faith, he arrived as a
foreigner, in the promised land, and lived there as if
in a strange country with Isaac and Jacob, who were
heirs with him of that same promise. They lived there
in tents while he looked forward to a city founded,
designed and built by God (Heb 11:8-10).

Ten years ago I was a photographer, working in New
York City and New Jersey photo studios. My title was photo illustrator, and my job description included setting up
and photographing merchandise for advertising in news-
papers, magazines, catalogues and television.

I thought I had everything. My job paid well. I had
money to buy anything that I wanted, and I went out every
night and enjoyed all of the "wine, women and song" that
anyone could have imagined. I really believed that I could
have anything I wanted. My friends all looked up to me
because I was successful and "had made it." But the truth
persisted—my life was shallow.

My goal in life was to promote products for sale, make someone a lot of money, and in return be rewarded for my good work. My sales philosophy sounded like: "Buy this and be happy," or: "You have not made it till you own one of these." I pushed consumers to "keep up with the Joneses." I knew all of the "tricks of the trade" to get their attention and stimulate their desires. My "friends" were around to have a good time. Yet, if I really needed someone, no one was there.

Several years ago I found out what life was truly about. I discovered why we were born into this world. I came to experience the God that I was told about by my parents and taught about during the thirteen years of Catholic schooling: the gentle and loving Father, the merciful and forgiving Son, and the powerful and ever-present Holy Spirit. God was calling me for many years, but I was too busy with myself to be involved with him.

I finally received his message through a true friend. Jesus was alive to her. The Holy Spirit was working in and through her to touch me. I said "yes" to God. I remember saying: "Here I am. I'm yours. Send me." When we say "yes" to God, he knows just what to do with us.

After being involved in my local parish prayer group and various ministries there, I moved to southwestern Georgia. There I volunteered full-time as a photographer and darkroom technician for an ecumenical Christian housing ministry called "Habitat for Humanity." I began to work with the materially poor. I saw and documented how many of our "brothers and sisters" lived in substandard conditions. I believed that my ability to sensitize people to the needs of others as a photographer was important and worthwhile. Yet there was still something missing.

As I spoke to many of these people, I recognized they

had a far greater need. Yes, they needed decent housing and fair-paying jobs to support their families, and, yes, they needed affordable medical care and proper diets, but they needed more than that. They needed to experience God in their lives. Working together in building a house can be an open door to share our experience of God. That is why I came to LAMP and now serve as a LAMP minister in Harlem, at St. Charles Borromeo Church on West 141st Street in New York City. The community is struggling to rebuild its neighborhood. Many of the people here recognize the need for change. My new parish family is rich in cultural heritage and very strong in faith. They have reached out to me and made me feel welcome in my new home.

Together, as a faith community, we are reaching out to others and sharing the daily experience of God in our lives. My role as a LAMP minister is taking some time to develop here at St. Charles. I've been commissioned as a eucharistic minister, enabling me to bring Jesus in the Blessed Sacrament to those in the hospital and home-bound. We are also working to start a new music ministry in the parish to enhance our Saturday evening liturgies. I am looking forward to beginning a home visiting program which my pastor sees as a great need in our parish.

My main involvement so far has been with our school and C.C.D. children. I almost forgot how the world looks through the eyes of a ten year old. It gets pretty rough around here in the neighborhood sometimes, and there are so many choices that these children must make every day. Being a LAMP minister here is allowing me to be a positive influence and role model for the young people. Yes, sometimes their stomachs may be empty, but they also have a real hunger for God. They have so many questions, and I am so glad that I am there to talk with them.

Ten years ago I promoted "Buy! Buy! Buy! and Get Happy." Three years ago, I told people, "Give! Give! Give! Make someone else happy." Today I ask you, "Come with me on a journey! Receive God! Experience him and share with others what he provides you with." Together, you and I, as pilgrims, are sent out to a country, founded, designed and built on God. This is our inheritance. Let's invite everyone we meet along the way.

"JUST WHAT I WAS LOOKING FOR!"
Maureen Hogan

LAMP Minister Maureen Hogan is from St. Lucy's Parish in the Bronx.

I grew up in an average Irish-American family in a middle class neighborhood in New Jersey. My parents are wise people who brought my brother and me up with a healthy sense of the church and the distinction between right and wrong. As I grew up, I was fooled into believing the many lies of the devil that are affecting society today. I looked to other people and material things to find fulfillment. I spent my high school years searching for happiness, and continually I was coming up empty.

When I was seventeen I was invited to a youth conference at Franciscan University in Steubenville, Ohio. For the first time in my life I began to look at Jesus and my Catholic upbringing as a source of joy and fulfillment. But for the next two years of my life I continued to spend myself on worldly ambitions.

When I was nineteen the Lord revealed to me on a retreat that to experience the abundant life he desired for me, I had to see all else as naught. I had to put him first and surrender my life to him. The next few years were a wonderful time of growth and transformation for me. With each passing day the Lord helped me to see more and more of his truth and his love for me. This new life I was living brought me more happiness than I ever thought possible.

Before too long I realized that God was calling me to serve him full-time. I found out about NET (National Evangelization Teams), a Catholic youth retreat team. I spent fifteen months working on a team of twelve people, sharing my faith with young people in the U.S. and Australia. While I was on NET, the Lord started to give me a real burden for the poor. It seemed that everywhere I looked he was surrounding me with literature, experiences, and scripture readings concerning the poor. I fought it for a long time. It took me a good year or so before I could share with my closest friends what I felt God was calling me to do.

Working with the poor was foreign to me. Up until this time I lived a materialistic Christian life. I had enough outfits to clothe all of Ethiopia. I never deprived myself of anything I wanted that was within my reach. I never thought too much about the poor. I didn't grow up seeing many materially poor people, and when I did I just thought of them as "bums" or "losers." As my relationship with Jesus deepened, I was forced to look at the type of life Jesus led. Jesus willingly chose to be poor. I began to examine the effects of all the "things" in my life. It wasn't hard to see how they crippled me. As I concentrated on living a simpler life I began to experience the tremendous freedom that accompanies it. And as I reflected on the poor of this world today, it was easier to say "no" to the new dress or the new cassette tape.

From this point I knew I was called to continue in full-time evangelization but now it would be with the poor. But when? Where? How? I saw an ad for LAMP Ministries in *New Covenant* magazine. "A Catholic Evangelization Ministry serving the materially poor"—just what I was looking for! And so close to home too! I've been a LAMP minister for a few months now. I am serving at St. Lucy's Parish in the Bronx. I am involved mainly in youth and young adult ministries. St. Lucy's is a very big and busy parish. There are many needs here. It gives me great joy to be able to aid the staff in meeting those needs as a LAMP minister.

Since November I've had many opportunities to go out on LAMP's Manna truck, feeding and evangelizing the hungry poor, to visit families in a welfare hotel, and to spend time with other LAMP ministers and those they serve. The poor continue to teach me so much about freedom and true happiness. So many of the poor have such strong relationships with the Lord. They easily recognize their need for God. Clearly one can "see Christ" in their faces, a paradox of paradoxes. I thank God for opportunities to be with the poor, to learn from them. And I thank God for a ministry like LAMP, that makes it possible for me to serve God full-time as a lay person.

A Closer Look

A WORD FROM LAMP YOUTH

Maria ("Mia") Scheuring:

Serving the poor with my family for almost fifteen years now is something that has practically become second nature to me. Beginning at age six, with our venture to Juarez, Mexico, we spent two months giving food, support and the love of God to the poverty stricken, living in what seemed to be miles of dumps and shacks of mud and cardboard. Two years later we moved to San Antonio, Texas. At the age of eight I was slightly oblivious as to my parents' objectives, but always felt a certain peace and happiness by just being able to bring a spark of joy into these people's lives. About that time my parents told us of the vision of LAMP. Being ten at that time, I didn't totally understand what they were trying to explain, and even then (though not admitting it at the time) I thought it to be a bit "far-fetched."

Upon our move to the Bronx, I began to see the sparks of their vision igniting. Although beginning in a very small way, my younger sister and brother and I tried to lend our support in their determination to make this a reality. Aside from the beginnings of LAMP Ministries, we continued ministering as a family to the urban poor.

By going down to Manhattan's lower East Village (the "Bowery") frequently, I saw first-hand poverty that was right under my nose the whole time. Often depicted in our society as "bums," "derelicts" or "prostitutes," I be-

gan to see them as "real people," "special" people, people
God put on the earth for an individual purpose, just as he
did with us. They are special because our society has
brainwashed people into thinking that they just "clutter
the streets," labeling their surroundings as "bad neighborhoods," and most of us do everything we can to "avoid
the sight of them." Why? This was a recent realization that
occurred to me, probably from a consciousness of growing up, being taught that all people are equal and should
be treated just the way we wish to be treated, as Jesus
himself taught. I thought: "After all, isn't that the ideal in
which our country prides itself also?"

At this time, I felt that if *I* could serve the poor, even
at ten or eleven years of age, why couldn't other children
my age? So LAMP's associate director, Marybeth, my sister
Malissa, and I began Lamplighters, the youth outreach of
LAMP Ministries. The purpose we had in mind was to become a Christian support to other youths while also encouraging them to serve the needy in more tangible and
concrete ways. We planned and organized monthly Saturday afternoon get-togethers, which usually included a
short film on a particular saint, or a brief skit to teach
Christian values. We would then have some discussion and
an activity, such as making rosaries, the Mexican "Eye of
God" cross, and plaques, or writing letters to prisoners. It
was understood, however, that everything that was made
would go directly to the poor and needy through the
LAMP ministers.

As I reached high school age, I and the other "senior"
Lamplighters helped to direct and assist at these monthly
meetings, but we began another outreach on our own.
Going to welfare hotels for homeless families, shelters, or
the Bowery, we physically served the homeless through
clown ministry, distributing food or clothing and the arti-

cles made by the Lamplighters, yet strived to keep in mind
the primary purpose of our mission: to show Jesus' love
for them in the midst of their seemingly destitute lives.
The closest identification which developed was most especially with the children and teenagers. It was amazing
how similar they are to us, as we learned through our discussions and interactions with them, yet they remain such
outcasts in our society.

Now, a college student at the age of twenty, I aim to
make a regular habit of visiting welfare hotels, shelters
and work on Manna (LAMP's mobile soup kitchen) whenever I am home. Going to school at Franciscan University
in Steubenville, Ohio, at first seemed far removed from
"the city poor" I was used to seeing, but I've come to
realize the different types of poverty that are evident all
around us, even if we may not be aware of it at the time. I
and my sorority sisters are beginning to lend our services,
love and even just an ear to local soup kitchens, homes for
unwed mothers, and children in welfare housing.

As I look back on my life so far, and all the exposure I
have had to the harsh reality of poverty and the opportunities to serve, I realize that the poor have taught me more
than I feel I would ever be able to give them. Being human,
I sometimes wasn't too zealous about spending my Saturdays in ghettos and on the streets, but there is nothing in
the world that could ever replace the tremendous peace
and joy I feel when a smile radiates out of one poverty
marked face of a child.

Malissa Scheuring:

Poverty—so much encompassed in such a simple
word, which touches every aspect of life. I am involved in
and admire those who work with the poor. This involvement with the poor, homeless and needy is an experience

that has had a profound impact on my personal development. When I can bring just one smile to a face, I am filled with great joy and happiness.

From a young age I have worked with the poor in various places, such as Mexico and Texas where my family and I resided for about two years. At that time in my life I thought it was everyone's second nature to help those in need, but as I have grown I have realized that that is not the case at all. I have found that many people in today's society look with disdain upon those who have less than they. What I have come to discover is that frequently those who possess the most materially are those who really have little, yet those who possess little often have such an inner richness.

For the past eleven years, I have been involved with LAMP Ministries and Lamplighters, the youth outreach. Together with my family and those who ministered with us, I have seen what others have tried to ignore: the poor outcasts sleeping in the doorways, the children naked and hungry, mothers holding onto the lives they have brought forth, fathers searching for food and maybe a piece of cardboard to build a shelter for those they love.

These sights draw something out of me which is inexplicable. I feel a strong compassion which calls me to reach out. The poor are so simple, yet are able to share such great joy. Their love comes so freely—seemingly unconditional. The poverty I've encountered has greatly affected me. It has strengthened me as a person, as well as those values and beliefs which I allow to guide me down my life's road. It has opened my eyes to the selfishness and greed which makes us so poor, and the love and simplicity whose richness is beyond comprehension.

With each day of my life, this, what I believe to be true, sinks deeper into my heart. At this writing I sit here at my summer lifeguarding job, among the wealthy, and I feel somewhat "in awe" of their way of life—their yachts, their Jaguars, their clothing and chains of gold. I sometimes dream of what it would be like to be just like them— to have such a life of leisure where any possession is within reach. But the more I look at their faces, the more I begin to wonder. Their wrinkles obviously aren't of age, but seemingly of worry or anguish, true happiness left undiscovered. The wants of the wealthy are never ending; rather they continue to grow. Then I look at the housing projects for low income families, located across the canal from where the yachts are docked. The contrast is frightening. I sometimes wonder what my life would be like if I too were wealthy. It would appear that my life would be set—but that is the farthest thing from the truth. Of course money has its momentary pleasure, but I've come to experience that "momentary" is exactly what it is. God's love, on the other hand, never ceases to exist. St. Thérèse really seemed to understand his love. It is always there whether the sun is shining or the clouds are covering the big blue sky. We can only have faith and hope in this reality, since it isn't tangible. It goes far beyond the love we have or ever will experience, and this is the richness we have yet to discover.

I now pray and always will pray that with every decision I make, I will take a step on the right path of my journey. At this stage in my life, I often feel confused as to what to do with what God has given me. I do hope and, with trust, believe that the wrinkles I'll have will be from the great big smile on my face which has its roots in my heart.

Maria Asedillo:

I think my whole experience with LAMP has affected my life tremendously. Not only has it touched my life, it has touched other lives as well. LAMP's projects in the name of God have greatly benefited the less fortunate people.

In Manna a group of us LAMP youth help distribute food and the word of God to the hungry people on the streets of the Bronx. When I travel to Manhattan to college and work, I see many homeless and hungry people on the streets and in the subways. It hurts to see it because it's difficult to help each one of them on my own. Manna makes me feel as if I am doing something about these hungry people in the streets. And a good thing about Manna is that it provides some reading material about God that will hopefully serve as an inspiration of hope for some of these people who may find their lives empty.

Kristen Murphy:
I feel that all human beings go through cycles when they are growing up. First, we are young people, then young adults, and, finally, adults. I think that as we grow physically and mentally we must also grow spiritually. Manna has been such a big part of my experiences with the poor and others who are oppressed, like prisoners and the elderly. Lamplighters has been a good experience. It was fun and I never was forced to go—I wanted to go. We make projects, not to take home, but for the poor. We wanted to do our best because we learned to think about others.

Once, while with Manna, I remember one family who came with a baby in a carriage and a little boy. The father was out of work but they were very friendly and appreciative. They were very loving toward each other.

More recently, there was a woman named Bonnie who came. It was winter, and she was feeling the cold. I gave her some warm clothes that I had brought. She said,

"This is like Christmas!" She then told me of how she used to be a prostitute, and of her hardships. No one ever spoke so honestly about one's personal life to me before.

I can't imagine my life without LAMP. Eight years is almost half of my life. Manna makes me more aware and more appreciative, yet angry when I hear that others are ignorant in talking about the poor. If they could spend time with them, they would know the real truth.

Everything that has happened through LAMP is proof of God's love—it makes me glad to be a believer. Doing all these things: Lamplighters, retreats, Manna—why would LAMP ministers do this unless there was a God telling them to do it? Helping someone without expecting anything in return really lets you see God. It is done in Jesus' name and it always stays with us.

Michael Keane:

When I first "joined" Lamplighters I was a young person who wanted to do his forty-eight hours of community service so that I could be confirmed into the Catholic Church. Lamplighters offered me the opportunity and I gladly accepted. We performed what was called "Clown Ministry" for deaf children. For me this was a shock. It was the first time in my life that I experienced how much joy one person can give to another person. These were children who couldn't speak or hear, yet they seemed like the happiest people in the world.

That year I received confirmation, and I figured that was it with the Lamplighters. Little did I know that about a week or so later I would receive a phone call from Marybeth, saying that they were going to perform the clown ministry again and asking me if I would like to take part in it. Needless to say, I did. This time we went to a hotel for the homeless in Times Square, Manhattan. I have to admit that I was a little nervous. It was great! Once again, here was a group who had nothing—I mean absolutely nothing, not even a home—and yet it seemed as if they were as happy as could be. They hugged us, thanked us, prayed with us, and told us their life stories.

I had never been so confused, mainly for two reasons. The first one was that in school they teach us about religion and the church. To be honest, I didn't find any of it very interesting. Meanwhile, here I was acting out scenes from the Bible, dressed as a clown and loving every minute of it. The second reason I was confused was because I felt that these people we were reaching out to had nothing, yet they seemed as happy as they could be.

Now that I look back, I see that religion and the church isn't just something you learn in school, it's a way of life. It's reaching out to people and showing them the goodness that exists in the world, the goodness of God. Lamplighters showed me that people who appear to have nothing frequently have more to offer than people who have everything. These homeless people and the handicapped are just examples of how love can shine much more than physical possessions.

I think the main reason I am thankful toward Lamplighters is because they gave me guidance as I went from a young person to a young adult and now hopefully to an adult. They showed me the importance of giving your love to someone else and the great satisfaction that can be received just by giving a homeless person on the street something to eat, or by just saying "hello" to someone who is down on life. I hope I can carry on the message I was taught by Lamplighters: "Love your neighbor today, tomorrow, next week, next year, and for the rest of your life."

Robert Kahwaty:

Manna has been my strongest experience with Lamplighters. It enables my friends and me to share with the poor—this idea of "sharing with" is what I think Jesus wants us to experience. We are not giving "to" the needy or providing "for" the poor, but we are sharing ourselves "with" the poor. In sharing, we too are enriched by the lives which momentarily touch ours. It is a two-way street: not only do we graciously have the chance to help the poor, but in sharing with them we become "the poor" depending on God. For me, depending on God is the core of my faith.

Paul Scheuring:

Throughout the years with Lamplighters, and now recently senior Lamplighters, I've discovered so much. I've found out that the saying "Don't judge a book by its cover" is so real. The people I've met during the times I've given out food, clothes, and drinks with the Manna outreach are more than nice. They come up to you and start talking as if they were good friends whom you've known for years. I guess it's because they are more free and the people have less to worry about, so they are happy with what they have.

Every time I go with the Manna truck, I see a poor man named Jim. He has become a friend. We talk to each other about his life. Whenever he needs clothes, he asks me and I try to find some that fit him, if we've brought clothes on the truck that day. Even though it seems that we come from different worlds because he is poor, it doesn't really matter if one of us is poor or not. The only thing that matters is that we are friends and that God loves us equally. So we should treat everyone equally.

I've also realized that homelessness is a problem which cannot be solved just by saying, "This has to stop." Action has to be taken. People always say, "We need to help them," and then they wait for others to do it. They don't realize that it's all of us who have to help to solve the problem. The problem could be solved but we all have to take part, for this is the only way.

Michele Lignore:
LAMP Ministries means a lot of things for a lot of different people. For me, the name LAMP itself signifies a beacon of God's light that brings people out of darkness.

In the few years that I've participated with Lamplighters, I have seen the eyes of young and old alike beam with happiness when LAMP offers its love, guidance, and support. They try to feed the poor and mistreated not only with food, but also with the message that God loves them.

I did clown ministry with Lamplighters at St. Joseph's School for the Deaf in the Bronx and at various homeless shelters in Manhattan. Through clown ministry we were able to extend God's love in a way that the children and others could understand. Many of the older people we performed for had little or no education due to their handicaps or lack of money. We chose stories from the Bible and made them into skits. The skits turned out to be enjoyable for everyone, ourselves and the audience. We also collected clothes from people throughout our area to give to the needy. We made homemade cards and rosaries to give to the poor, elderly, and forgotten ones.

The most significant experience I had with Lamplighters was in April 1988. Around Eastertime a group of us painted Easter eggs for the children of the Martinique Hotel in Manhattan. The Martinique is a very large welfare hotel for homeless families. Along with the eggs, we brought oranges, doughnuts, and small scripture readings to show them that God does not forget the poor. We emphasized that they are blest more than the richest of people. ("Blest are the lowly, the kingdom shall be theirs" was one of the beatitudes we stressed.)

That day in April was the very first time I visited the Martinique Hotel. I was apprehensive about going at first because I was afraid of what I would discover. Would the homeless people be scared of us the way we were scared of them? What am I going to say to a person who is homeless when I've had a nice home all my life? Are the homeless people going to steal or panhandle from us? These were just a few of the questions that were racing through my mind.

When we reached the hotel, we noticed drug dealers, bag ladies, and the like. At first I was afraid to enter the building, leery of what we might find. The lobby was massive. The walls were caked with dirt. But underneath all the filth, we could tell that it must have been a beautiful place once.

The majestic ceiling caught our attention, and as we were looking up at it we noticed that people were gathering to look at us. We saw the masses of young faces withered in sadness. Some of these children had never even had a coat of their own. They never had a decent home. Many were wearing old, worn T-shirts and little else. When we approached them to say "hello," they backed away because it was perhaps the first time they may have received a friendly greeting. We then made our journey up the stairs. That was the longest flight of stairs I ever climbed, only because I did not know what was waiting for me at the top.

Eventually we reached a dim area where the lights had been broken. We waited there while the tenants assembled to eat their next meal. The doors to the adjacent room, where the lunch was going to be served, were locked. The people were becoming impatient—many had not eaten since the previous day, but we mingled with the crowd and spread the good news nonetheless.

The first person I met was a little boy named Artie. Artie was seven years old, but he acted like an adult. He had no childhood, and was forced to grow up fast in his world. Artie explained how he lived there with his parents and an older brother. His large vocabulary surprised me because he lived in such squalid conditions. With all the influences and pressures around him, one would think that he would be overcome by them. Yet Artie appeared to be a strong young man. He wanted a better life for himself and his family, so he was ready to do what it took. He told me how lucky I was to have a home and that his dream was to have a home of his own one day. I was very touched by Artie because I never quite realized how different lives could be from one neighborhood to another. He made me value my home, my parents, my family, and my education more than I ever did before, and I thank God for it. I had gone to the hotel to help someone, but I was the one to receive the help that would last a lifetime.

If you ever have an opportunity to work with LAMP, you should grab it. Believe me, just one day can affect both you and the person you'll care about.

"BEING WITH" THE HOMELESS

Works of the Spirit

One day, one of the LAMP ministers (LM) who serves in a welfare hotel for homeless families shared at our regular Monday meeting about a number of new homeless families that had moved into the hotel. She had met about eighteen new families in recent weeks. Among them there were over fifty children and adults that were being connected to the local parish for religious instruction, reception of the sacraments, marriages, etc. If the LM wasn't there, this connection would not have been made. Previous to LAMP's presence in these shelters there was no way to connect these people to the supportive environment of the church. What a privilege it is for us to be instruments in this service of evangelization, of people coming to know and love the Lord more deeply.

Another shared experience helps show clearly the purpose of LAMP. A Catholic family, who came into one of the shelters for homeless families where a LM serves, seemed to be doing well when they arrived. However, over the days and weeks that followed, the LM, who had come to know them, saw the mother regress in many ways. When the LM came back from being away for a week, she saw the woman and was shocked by her condition. She had lost so much weight and looked terrible. She began to talk with the LM and told her that a few days earlier she was planning to commit suicide. She just couldn't take life and all its pain any longer. She was actually at the very moment of slashing her own wrists when, for some reason unknown to her, the words of the LM came into her mind about the love of God for her and his mercy. This caused her to stop her attempt at suicide and have hope in the midst of her situation and the courage to keep going. She thanked the LM for what really were "words of life."

A mother in a welfare hotel had been having a serious problem with her throat for a number of months. It swelled up and made it almost impossible to eat. She had lost very much weight. The doctor said that was caused by anxiety. At one point this woman shared her problem with one of the LAMP ministers serving in that hotel. The woman said that she was ready to give up on life. The LM talked to her and then wanted to pray for her that that condition would go away. The woman at first resisted being prayed with but eventually gave in. The next day, that woman came back to the LM all excited and giving thanks to God because she had been healed.

In many ways we have experienced the poor evangelizing us. When we see their faith in the midst of such desperate situations, it cannot help but call us forth to be more committed to Jesus ourselves. There is a particular SRO (single room occupancy) hotel in the Times Square area at which LAMP ministers have been serving for a number of years. This hotel is not only a shelter for homeless mothers and their children, but many elderly live there, trying to survive on what government assistance they can get, having lived for various lengths of time on the street or for a time in a mental institution. Many of these senior citizens are totally broken people. They weren't always this way, but circumstances in their lives have caused them to be totally alone, with little chance of a way out.

Jennie used to be an opera singer. She now lives in this Times Square hotel. She is afraid to go to the basement where the clothes washers are for fear of being mugged. She is forced to wear the few clothes she has until she can't stand the smell or they wear out. It is hard for us to imagine the life of people who have no choices or options.

Daisy, another woman at that hotel tells us: "I don't know God very much. I just know he loves me." We say to ourselves, "What more is there?"

A LAMP minister, who serves in a welfare hotel for homeless families, is spending a couple of days each week visiting some families in their "new" rundown apartment, to which they were moved when one of the hotels closed. One of the families, whom the LM had gotten to know well, had a ten year old daughter who would always run up to the LM in the hotel, put her arms around her and tell her, "I want to be like you!" Recently this LM was going to visit this family at their apartment, and when she was still walking down the street approaching the apartment building, the little girl saw her coming and ran to her, threw her arms around her and said: "I want to be like you." This girl was attracted by something. In the midst of all of our weakness and inadequacy, we know that what attracted that girl was God himself.

One day, I (Tom) was visiting some rooms of homeless families living in one of the shelters, with Ed Greene, the LM who serves in that shelter. We went into one of the rooms where a mother lives with her four children. Actually she was very happy because they had two small rooms.

My attention was drawn to a ripped piece of paper taped on the wall which had about three scripture references handwritten on it. One reference had the passage written next to it. It read: "We live by faith, not by sight" (2 Cor 5:7). The homeless mother commented on what a deep passage that was. Obviously she knew the reality of that passage more than most of us.

Joe Tysz, an LM, served half-time in a very poor parish in Yonkers and the other half-time with homeless families in that same area. One day, through a donation to LAMP, he was able to arrange for a teenager from one of the homeless families to go on a weekend spiritual retreat. She, and a couple of other teenagers from homeless families, were also beginning to come and meet with the youth group which Joe had begun in the parish where he served.

A few days after she had returned from the retreat there was a parish youth meeting. At the meeting Joe asked this particular girl to read for everyone that scripture passage about how Jesus tells us to love our enemies (Mt 5:43–48). She read it very clearly and convincingly. After the meeting, she came to Joe and told him that she had been asked to read that same passage at the retreat but wasn't able to read it. Joe asked her why she was able to read it now. She replied: "Jesus touched my heart with his love at the retreat, and now I am free to read it." She also told him: "When I returned from the retreat, I went to visit my father. While we were talking, he told me that he loved me. That was the first time that he had ever said that to me."

Sr. Judith serves as an LM in a parish in the South Bronx. Recently a homeless woman was rummaging through a dumpster on one of the side streets near the church. Another woman came by and asked the woman what she was doing. The homeless woman responded that she was looking for some clothes for her children. The other woman immediately said that she should go to Sr. Judith in the parish.

Sr. Judith had a very good visit with her, prayed with her, and arranged for her to get some clothes and help for other needs the family had. She also began making arrangements for her children to attend religious instruction classes in the parish. The woman herself expressed an interest in being an active member of the parish, so Sr. Judith is arranging different areas where she can be of help. She has had one or two more opportunities to meet with her since that initial visit.

This family is being drawn into the parish faith community, their whole lives are being changed, and their children as well as the mother are being nurtured in the faith, all because a parishioner cared enough to inquire about this homeless woman looking through the garbage and was aware of the outreach of a LAMP minister in her parish.

We are all very familiar with the phrase from John's first letter where he says that "God is love." Sometimes phrases like that become so common that they lose their meaning. Recently one of the LAMP ministers experienced the power of love in communicating the gospel message even when very few words are said.

Ed and Julio (two LAMP ministers) were visiting a woman in a shelter for homeless families. She seemed to have so much anger in her toward God and the church. Many years ago she had stopped going to church. Her image of God was someone very mean, commenting that she had never seen a picture of God "laughing." They just listened without being defensive and made comments as they thought they should, trying to show love to the woman. A few days later Julio came across a picture of Jesus smiling, so he bought it, and the next time he went with Ed to visit at the shelter he brought the picture and gave it to the lady. She was very happy with that picture and grateful for their thoughtfulness. Ed had also mentioned this experience to other LAMP ministers. One of them, Bob, came across a picture of Jesus laughing and thought of this lady Ed had told him about, so he bought it (it was inexpensive) and gave it to Ed to give to the woman. She was so touched by their love that she began to be open to their sharing about Jesus. She expressed her desire to return to church and also wanted to make a retreat. She had made one many years earlier. This makes us very aware of how our love can touch lives with the gospel message even when our words don't.

On a particular day a LAMP minister serving in another welfare hotel for homeless families was sitting by his makeshift desk in the lobby of the hotel where he would visit with the residents. Homeless families can only stay a maximum of four weeks in this hotel, which sometimes makes the LM question if that is enough time to have any effect on the people. This one afternoon about four or five young children came around to visit him. Quite spontaneously he began a little class teaching them how to pray. He taught them the sign of the cross and how to pray to Jesus and with each other. After a period of time they left to go and play but shortly came back all excited, exclaiming: "We prayed together! We prayed together!" It became clear: no time is too short to lead someone to Jesus.

CONCLUSION

There is a challenging and convicting passage near the end of Matthew's gospel (Mt 25:31-46). It has to do with the last judgment and whether or not we recognized Jesus in the poor. After Jesus was asked when we saw him hungry, thirsty, naked, ill or imprisoned, he replied: "As often as you did it for one of my least, you did it for me." Those are very confronting words of Jesus.

These words of Jesus, identifying persons with himself, bring to mind an experience I (Lyn) had last December 1, the day after St. Andrew's feast. I had gone with some of the LAMP ministers and Lamplighters on the Manna outreach. Just as we were beginning to close for the day, a destitute man came hobbling over to the Manna truck for something to eat. He was poverty-worn, and obviously high on some alcohol and drugs. His eyes were filled with anger, distraught because someone had just beaten him and robbed him of the little he had. As I handed him a small bag of food and a cup of coffee, I asked him his name. He said: "My name is Andrew!" I told him: "Yesterday was the feast of St. Andrew." With a surprised look, he then began narrating his life story—growing up as a Catholic, how he had been an altar boy, about all the priests he knew, the schools he attended, etc. He then shared some of the hard times he had experienced. After his story and as he was beginning to leave, I asked him if he

would say a prayer for us, hoping he would remember to
do it as he was walking or if we came to his mind later in
the day. Instead, he immediately put down his bag of food
and cup of coffee on the sidewalk, folded his hands, reverently bowed his head and with closed eyes, uttered a
prayer—so profound and universal—caring about people
who suffer, asking God's blessing on all people. The LAMP
staff gathered around him and entered into his every word
to God. Surely we were convinced that this "poor man's
prayer pierced the clouds."

When Andrew finished his prayer, he opened his eyes,
now peace-filled and calm, looked at all of us and exclaimed: "You people make me feel so comfortable." He
paused and repeated: "You people make me feel so comfortable," and then for a third time as he reverently walked
away. We became so aware of the transformative power of
God's peace in this person through prayer. In communicating with God, a person experiences his or her own
dignity in its highest form. Truly, Jesus' identification with
Andrew was quite transparent. But our challenge is to see
Jesus in every brother and sister, no matter how unlike
Jesus they may seem at the moment.

Recently we again became aware of how easy it is to
think we understand others and what makes them the way
they are, only to realize that we were mistaken in our pre-
sumptions and that we should have been more patient or
compassionate—truly living by faith that we are loving
Jesus in each person.

LAMP minister Sr. Judith was talking one day with a
very destitute homeless woman of the neighborhood who
was on drugs. This woman is frequently a cause of annoy-
ance to those around her. Sister has been trying for some
time to get her into a drug rehabilitation program. This
particular day Sister was confronting her with her drug

problem, trying to make her aware of its danger, when the woman responded: "I don't have a drug problem. I just take a little crack." Sister continued to listen, to allow the woman to talk, trying to patiently love her. Gradually the woman became more vulnerable and began to share some of her pain. Finally, in tears, the woman said that she had been with two of her children when they were shot and killed on the street. "No matter how many showers I take, I can't wash away their blood on me as I held them dying."

What unbelievable agony lay buried in this mother's heart! It doesn't justify her use of drugs but it helps us to understand the cause and gives us more compassion, more motivation to keep loving, to find a way to meet the needs of the poor. It is so easy to put a superficial label on the poor and homeless. As we are able to see the suffering Jesus in these people's lives, we will be more disposed to listen to their stories, to stand with them, to pray with them, trusting the Lord to help find solutions.

The "personal love of Jesus" may be difficult to experience in times of suffering. However, when we do experience a specific awareness of the Lord's love, we also experience a freedom that nothing else can provide. There is a striking passage in the letter to the Galatians: "Freedom is what we have—Christ has set us free! Stand, then, as free people, and do not allow yourselves to become slaves again" (Gal 5:1).

We all know how easy it is to slip back into slavery, to any attachment which does not bring life. We are exhorted that it is only through a relationship with Jesus that we can be free of slavery. In LAMP, as the Holy Spirit works in us through contact with the poor, we often come to deeper realizations of the freedom that Jesus has in mind for us.

An example of this is a man who served for a year with LAMP a few years ago. Bob had been a computer science instructor for seven years. He was so caught up in that profession that it had almost become an obsession with him. He knew something had to change, that his life needed to be reoriented. Part of this process was his applying to LAMP, and then serving in a poor Bronx parish.

Some time ago Bob came back to visit us. He wanted to thank us for our part in the change that took place in his life while he was a LAMP minister. Through his formation in LAMP and his ministry in the parish, he came to a much deeper commitment to Jesus in his life. At one point, Bob had put it this way: "Living out the gospel, as a LAMP minister, is like walking under a great light. Sometimes that light exposes things in me that I'd rather not see, but on the positive side, that 'light' is a beautiful and ennobling reality. It is, of course, the light of God's wonderful love." When Bob left LAMP, he knew that he wanted to spend the rest of his life in a ministry of evangelization.

Bob shared with us that he now makes his living through caring for a parapalegic man, but has most of his day free. He spends this free time reaching out in an evangelistic ministry to the very poor who live in a SRO (single room occupancy) hotel, where he also lives. He still wears his LAMP cross (which all LAMP ministers receive when they become part of LAMP), and has such an air of peace and joy about him.

Through the grace of God, Bob has not allowed himself to become a slave again. He is very conscious of the fact that a very important component of holding onto the freedom of Christ is to give oneself in some form of service with the poor and being a witness to the good news.

This experience is also an example of how LAMP not only is instrumental in training people for evangelization with the poor, but also prepares them for a new life of service in the church after their service through LAMP ends. It is the prayers and financial assistance of those who support LAMP that make possible this ministry of evangelization with the materially poor, but it also is helping to form Christian leaders who will continue to be strong and effective channels of God's love when they leave this particular ministry.

The witnesses contained in this book may at times be misleading. It can make this ministry seem so easy, and/or always successful. This isn't the case. Loneliness, disappointing results, failed attempts, are also part of a missionary's call and something we also experience. The drama and excitement of the ministry carries a LAMP minister through the difficult moments of the first few months, but that stage may soon wear away and the commitment to the Lord, his personal call to each one of us, and loving his people no matter what, has to take over as the sole reason for undertaking such a challenging ministry.

Even though this is the end of the book, the journey continues. In poverty of spirit we press on, praying that we be faithful to the Spirit's unfolding vision for this, *his* LAMP—and for you in your gospel call, whichever way the Spirit may be leading you.

We rely on our common community—the communion of saints—who have stood with us in this venture and to whom we look for intercession:

Mary, mother of the church and Our Lady of LAMP, pray for us;

St. Joseph, faithful provider and patron of the universal church, pray for us;

St. Thérèse and St. Francis Xavier, patrons of missionaries, pray for us;

St. Francis and St. Clare, who lived poor for Christ, pray for us;

St. Martin de Porres, pray for us;

St. Anthony, pray for us;

Archangels St. Michael, St. Gabriel (patron of evangelizers), and St. Raphael, and also guardian angels, please protect and pray for us.

We thank our Father for all the saints and all those poor, hidden ones, who have gone before us marked with the sign of faith. May we always follow their example of looking to you. "For God, who said, 'Let light shine out of darkness,' has shone in our hearts, that we in turn might make known the glory of God shining on the face of Christ. This treasure we possess in earthen vessels, to make it clear that its surpassing power comes from God and not from us" (2 Cor 4:6-8).

For more information on LAMP please contact LAMP Ministries or this publisher.

LAMP Ministries
2704 Schurz Ave.
Bronx, NY 10465